D0845201

CORNELL STUDIES IN INDUSTRIAL AND LABOR RELATIONS NUMBER 24

SELF-EMPLOYMENT

A LABOR MARKET PERSPECTIVE

BOWLING GREEN STATE
UNIVERSITY LIBRARIES

ROBERT L. ARONSON

ILR PRESS
ITHACA, NEW YORK

BOWLING GREEN STATE UNIVERSITY DISCARDED LIBRARY

Copyright © 1991 by Cornell University
All rights reserved

Cover design by Susan Ulrich

Library of Congress Cataloging-in-Publication Data

Aronson, Robert Louis, 1917–
    Self-employment : a labor market perspective / Robert L. Aronson.
        p.   cm. — (Cornell studies in industrial and labor relations
    : no. 24)
    Includes bibliographical references and index.
    ISBN 0–87546–175–1 (alk. paper). — ISBN 0–87546–176–X
(pbk. : alk. paper).
    1. Self-employed—United States. 2. Self-employed. I. Title.
II. Series.
HD6072.6.U5A76   1991
331.12—dc20   91–10487
                                                        CIP

Copies may be ordered through bookstores or from

ILR Press
School of Industrial and Labor Relations
Cornell University
Ithaca, NY 14851–0952

Printed on acid-free paper in the United States of America

5 4 3 2 1

For Judith, Michal, and Elizabeth

Contents

Tables

Preface

Self-employment is unquestionably the oldest way by which individuals offer and sell their labor in a market economy. At an earlier time, it was also the primary way. Despite this history, its principal features and the characteristics that differentiate self-employment from wage and salary employment have attracted the attention of only a handful of students of the labor market. Consequently, it has yet to be incorporated to any significant extent into the literature of industrial relations research and analysis.

Prior to this study, only two other studies attempted to delineate the nature of self-employment as a labor market phenomenon. One of these (Phillips 1962) brought together data on the employment and earnings of the nonfarm self-employed between the interwar period and the post–World War II years up to 1960. Although in most instances that study did not compare the self-employed with wage and salary workers, its findings implicitly raised issues that might have attracted the interest of labor economists and other industrial relations specialists. Unfortunately, this did not occur, possibly because the publication escaped the attention of the scholarly community.[1] The other study (Leveson 1968), despite its stronger analytical orientation, virtually vanished into obscurity, as happens to many doctoral dissertations.

The main objective of this study is to remove self-employment from its obscurity and thereby encourage others in the academic community to ex-

---

1. Phillips's study and a related earlier work (Phillips 1958) were both published as monographs in paperback only. This could have led to their failure to be reviewed in leading journals. More likely, self-employment was not only declining but overshadowed by the more dramatic events associated with the growth of organized labor that in part gave impetus to the development of industrial and labor relations in its initial years as a field of academic study.

amine its features as a significant labor market phenonemon. I have tried to accomplish this in two ways. First, I have searched for and organized data on the principal labor market dimensions of nonfarm self-employment: its relative share of civilian nonfarm employment, its rate of growth, its demographic and social composition, its industrial and occupational distributions, its relative earnings, and its institutional settings, especially in relation to government and public policy. On a number of these dimensions (but certainly far less than desired), data from other industrialized countries have been introduced to provide a comparison with developments in the United States.

Second, I have identified and used studies that analyze one or more of the labor market dimensions of nonfarm self-employment. I have confined my search for relevant literature to the nonfarm sector, although there is some literature on farming as self-employment, first, because self-employment has been growing in the nonfarm sector, and, second, because I wished to compare the nonfarm self-employed with wage and salary workers, who constitute about 90 percent of the nonfarm work force.

The studies on which I draw are principally from the fields of economics and sociology. In a majority of instances they were not designed to address questions usually covered in the analysis of labor market relationships, such as earnings variations and differentials or the dynamics of entry and exit in response to changes in the labor market. The majority of the studies addressed issues in which self-employment was thematically secondary. Several recent studies focused on nonfarm self-employment, however, and therefore provided exceptionally useful findings and insights on such issues. In addition to commenting throughout this book on the significance of the findings of all of these studies, I have tried in the final chapter to summarize systematically the state of our understanding of self-employment as a labor market phenomenon and to propose an agenda for further research.

Three developments account for my interest in self-employment and the self-employed. All of these developed with my immersion in the data sources and my literature search.[2] First and foremost is the reemergence of nonfarm self-employment as a substantial component of the labor force. This has occurred during the past two decades in the United States and concurrently in a number of other, but not all, countries at approximately

---

2. My initial interest came about through an effort to find for teaching purposes a literature on self-employed professional workers. The scarcity of such a literature motivated a broader search for material on self-employment as a labor market phenomenon.

the same stage of economic development. Whether this reemergence represents a structural change in the urban labor markets of industrially advanced countries or is the consequence of impermanent and transitory factors remains to be seen.

The second reason for my interest is that the growth of nonfarm self-employment has been accompanied in the United States and elsewhere by major shifts in the social and demographic composition of the self-employed. Compared with the pre–World War II and early postwar decades, self-employment is not as markedly dominated by middle-aged white males. Increasing numbers of women, especially, and members of some racial minorities are proprietors of their own businesses. These shifts have not only changed the face of self-employment but to some degree reflect broader social and cultural changes in the nature of work.

The third reason for my interest is that the behavior of nonfarm self-employment may challenge the standard models of the labor market. Those models generally are based on so-called hedonistic assumptions. Individuals behaving hedonistically are assumed to behave rationally in their employment decisions, that is, to maximize utility or satisfaction and minimize cost or pain. Although nonmonetary considerations can be embraced in such models, they are frequently ignored or are represented as coincident with the influence of money. The labor market behavior of the self-employed appears to contradict the logic of the standard models in a number of respects, suggesting in part that nonmonetary influences may carry greater weight in employment decisions. The recent growth of self-employment, for example, seems almost perverse viewed against the more favorable and growing earnings advantage of wage and salary workers. Specifically, the sharp rise in self-employment among women is difficult to explain given that their earnings, even when adjusted for differences in time worked, are well below those of women employees. These and other enigmas of self-employment are described and discussed in several of the chapters that follow.

The meaning and measurement of self-employment is itself something of an enigma, as readers of this study will discover. The general viewpoint here is that self-employment is basically an alternative means of earning a living by the sale of one's labor. As I hope the discussion emphasizes, most self-employed workers are not entrepreneurs in the classic sense, that is, individuals with a unique mission of breaking new ground in the production and/or distribution of goods and services. Rather, wisely or otherwise and for a variety of reasons, they have chosen to work for themselves. Accordingly, I have not ventured into the literature on entrepreneurship except to illuminate the employment and earnings of the self-employed.

The labor market orientation of this study has also led me to adopt to the degree feasible a narrow definition of who is self-employed. Some efforts to count the self-employed have included partners or unpaid family workers or both. These more inclusive definitions raise questions, however, about the degree of autonomy and control these workers have over their labor, which, in my view, theoretically distinguishes self-employment from wage and salary employment. Such definitions also imply different institutional contexts and, even more important, different responses to such labor market signals as relative earnings and employment opportunities. To distinguish self-employment from wage and salary employment, data sources permitting, I have excluded partners and unpaid family workers from employment estimates.

Counting the self-employed, as I discuss in the appendix, is always going to be subject to ambiguity for a number of reasons. Some otherwise useful data sources do not indicate the degree to which individuals are exclusively dependent on self-employment income. In addition, individuals involved in the "underground economy" may for obvious reasons be reluctant to identify their employment status to data collectors. Furthermore, the Bureau of the Census classifies the incorporated self-employed as wage and salary workers. Where information is available, I have treated them as self-employed.[3] Finally, there is a heterogeneous group, including commission salespersons and franchise holders, who may or may not be self-employed in a legal or contractual sense.

The last chapter proposes a research agenda on self-employment as a labor market phenomenon. I hope others will be stimulated by this book to enlarge on and/or modify these suggestions. The literature of the labor market and our understanding of its dimensions and behavioral patterns will remain seriously incomplete until more extensive research and analysis focused on self-employment are incorporated into that literature.

I very much appreciate the many authors whose work I have used in this study. I hope I have not misrepresented their efforts. A number of individuals have been directly helpful in various ways by supplying data, calling

---

3. Although the numbers and characteristics of incorporated self-employed are available in tape format, one wishes that the Bureau of the Census and the U.S. Department of Labor would return to the practice of identifying and providing some detail on the characteristics of this important group in its serial publications, such as *Employment and Earnings*.

my attention to literature that escaped my bibliographic search, providing me with their work in progress, and making useful comments on an early draft of this study. I gratefully acknowledge the help of Herbert Aronson, Steven Balkin, Ronald Ehrenberg, Robert Hutchens, Jules Lichtenstein, Roger Little, Ruth Spitz, and Udo Staber. I also very much appreciate the interest and care with which Erica Fox and Graham Leggat of ILR Press transformed the original manuscript into print.

SELF-EMPLOYMENT

CHAPTER ONE

The Reemergence
of Self-Employment

In 1962, after reviewing trends over the previous decades, economist Joseph D. Phillips, in his pioneering study of self-employment, characterized it as a "shrinking world within a growing economy" (1962). Although noting some exceptions, such as the independent professions and other personal service occupations, Phillips concluded that self-employment would survive principally as a defense against unemployment, albeit a poor one, or as a refuge for older workers, the physically and mentally handicapped, and others with low personal productivity.

This verdict conflicts with the popular portrait of self-employment, which is based to some degree on myths about our increasingly remote agrarian past. In that picture self-employment is a virtual synonym for individual freedom, independence of thought and action, and honest workmanship, usually accompanied by middle-class status and income. It is doubtful that reality ever exactly corresponded to the myth; regardless, industrialization has made self-employment an unrealizable goal for most American workers. As Chinoy (1955) described it in his study of industrial workers, the "American dream" of self-employment became more fantasy than reality.

Indeed, for the period covered by Phillips's study, 1929–60, both farm and nonfarm self-employment declined rapidly and sharply. In the nonfarm sector, the concern of this study, more than one of every four workers at the beginning of the century was self-employed. At the close of World War I, self-employment accounted for about 15 percent of nonfarm employment. Although nonfarm self-employment began to increase in absolute terms at the close of World War II, in relative terms the prewar decline continued.

1

By 1960, only one of every ten nonfarm workers was so employed,[1] and by 1970, estimated self-employment had declined to below 7 percent.

Early in the 1970s, however, the long-term decline halted and was replaced by growth at annual rates that often exceeded the rate of employment growth overall. Accompanying this reemergence of nonfarm self-employment were changes in some of its principal social and economic characteristics. In the following sections of this chapter, the trends and main dimensions of nonfarm self-employment since World War II are set forth. The trends in other industrialized countries are also described.

Nonfarm Self-Employment since World War II

Tracing the course of self-employment has long been an uncertain exercise, made difficult by inadequate demographic and labor market counting schemes and by ambiguity in the definition of self-employment itself. (For a discussion of measurement issues and data sources, see the appendix.) Despite differences in the estimated numbers of people engaged in nonfarm self-employment, however, the data from the principal sources support the same trend with relatively consistent timing. For the post–World War II period, I have chosen to use data from the records of employment covered under the Social Security law and from the income tax records of the Internal Revenue Service (IRS) on sole proprietorships. These appear to be the least contaminated by changes in definition and the hazards of self-reporting, which influence some Census and Current Population Survey (CPS) data, though as the appendix makes clear they have measurement problems of their own. None of these problems, however, obscures the principal trend.

Table 1.1 traces the growth of self-employment from 1955 to 1988.[2] From 1955 to 1970, the Social Security data show a general downward drift in absolute terms and a clear decline in relative terms. IRS data for the same period show virtually no growth in nonfarm sole proprietorships. Then, beginning in the early 1970s, self-employment began an almost spectacular revival. For example, in the 1972–76 period wage and salary employment increased by a little more than 6.5 percent while self-employment increased almost twice as fast. Census and Bureau of Labor Statistics (BLS)

---

1. Estimated from Lebergott 1964.
2. Social insurance coverage of self-employment did not begin in the United States until 1955.

TABLE 1.1. EMPLOYMENT, BY CLASS OF WORKER, SELECTED YEARS, 1955–1988 (in thousands)

Year	Wage and salary	Nonfarm self-employed	Self-employed as percentage of all workers	Sole proprietors
1955	59,560	6,680	10.4	–
1960	66,980	6,870	9.5	5,731
1965	75,430	6,550	8.1	6,015
1966	79,460	6,630	7.4	6,068
1967	82,020	6,470	7.4	6,096
1968	84,470	6,570	7.4	6,169
1969	87,200	6,350	6.9	6,340
1970	88,180	6,270	6.7	6,494
1971	88,460	6,290	6.7	6,803
1972	91,220	6,600	6.8	7,165
1973	94,610	7,100	7.1	7,445
1974	96,910	7,040	6.9	7,695
1975	94,900	7,000	7.0	7,759
1976	97,230	7,400	7.2	8,140
1977	100,450	7,480	7.1	8,414
1978	104,810	8,040	7.3	8,908
1979	106,900	8,200	7.4	9,344
1980	107,200	8,200	7.3	8,944
1981	107,450	8,300	7.3	9,345
1982	105,800	8,550	7.6	9,877
1983	105,900	9,200	8.0	10,500
1984	109,800[a]	9,700[a]	8.1	11,327
1985	113,300	10,300[a]	8.3	11,767
1986	115,900[a]	10,900[a]	8.6	12,115
1987	117,900[a]	11,300[a]	8.7	N.A.
1988	120,900[a]	11,600[a]	8.8	N.A.

SOURCES: Employment: U.S. Department of Health and Human Services 1989; sole proprietors: 1960–79, U.S. Treasury 1981; 1980–86, SBA, *State of Small Business, 1987.*
[a]Estimates subject to adjustment.

data confirm the trend (Fain 1980; Becker 1984; Steinmetz and Wright 1989), though they place the beginning of the upturn later in the decade. For the period 1955–86, however, the gain in wage and salary employment still exceeded the increase in self-employment. Wage and salary employment increased by about 97 percent while self-employment increased by 53 percent, or about half the rate of wage employment. IRS data on sole

TABLE 1.2.   WOMEN AS A PERCENTAGE OF EMPLOYMENT, BY CLASS
OF WORKER, SELECTED YEARS, 1955–1986 (in thousands)

Year	All workers	% Women	Self-Employed	% Women
1955	65,200	33.8	6,810	12.2
1960	72,530	33.9	6,870	12.8
1965	80,680	35.6	6,550	13.9
1970	93,090	38.4	6,270	14.3
1975	100,200	40.6	7,000	17.3
1976	102,600	41.2	7,400	18.4
1977	105,800	41.7	7,480	19.5
1978	110,600	42.2	8,040	20.4
1979	112,700	42.7	8,200	20.7
1980	113,000	43.1	8,200	21.9
1981	113,000	43.4	8,250	22.9
1982	111,800	43.6	8,550	24.6
1983	113,000[a]	43.9	9,300[a]	25.9
1984	117,500[a]	44.4	9,800[a]	27.8
1985	121,300[a]	44.8	10,200[a]	28.5
1986	124,500[a]	44.8	10,400[a]	28.5

SOURCE: U.S. Department of Health and Human Services, Social Security Administration,
Social Security Bulletin, Annual Statistical Supplement, 1988.
[a]Estimates subject to adjustment.

proprietorships, the great majority of which are single-person enterprises,
show a similar level and pattern of gain during the same period. For the
most recent five-year period, 1983–87, all data sources indicate a leveling-
off of the growth of self-employment and a return to the more stable pattern
of the 1960s (see U.S. Department of Labor 1988, *Labor Force Statistics*).

One element distinguishes the growth of self-employment during the late
1970s and early 1980s from earlier periods. During these recent decades,
the increase in nonfarm self-employment was led by women, who entered
self-employment at rates exceeding their rate into the labor force and nonfarm employment generally. There has been a steady increase in the share
of women in self-employment regardless of the annual changes in total nonfarm employment and in self-employment (table 1.2). For the entire period
1955–86, women increased their share of total employment by 29 percent,
while their share of self-employment increased by 113 percent. Data from
both the Social Security records and the Current Population Survey confirm
that the highest rates of entry of women began in the mid-1970s. Between
1975 and 1986, women accounted for 51 percent of the total gain in non-

TABLE 1.3. SELF-EMPLOYMENT RATES, BY GENDER, SELECTED YEARS, 1965–1986 (in thousands)

	Male		Female	
Year	Total	% self-employed	Total	% self-employed
1965	51,990	10.8	28,690	3.2
1970	57,330	9.4	35,760	2.5
1975	59,520	9.7	40,680	2.9
1978	63,960	10.0	46,460	3.5
1980	64,288	9.9	48,712	3.7
1982	63,089	10.2	48,711	4.3
1984	65,334[a]	10.9	52,166[a]	5.1
1986	68,718	10.8	55,782[a]	5.3

SOURCE: U.S. Department of Health and Human Services, Social Security Administration, *Social Security Bulletin, Annual Statistical Supplement, 1988.*
[a]Estimates subject to future adjustment.

farm self-employment, doubling their share at the beginning of that period. Until this time, the participation of women in nonfarm self-employment had followed the course of total self-employment, falling in both absolute and relative terms from the early 1940s until the period of rapid growth in the early 1970s.

Clearly, the increase in self-employment among women has had a major influence on the overall growth of nonfarm self-employment; however, this factor alone does not account for the entire increase. If one assumes, for instance, that the self-employment rate among women in 1975 remained unchanged in subsequent years, nonfarm self-employment would still have increased but at a slower rate. Thus, what is most important is that not only are self-employment rates among men more than twice those of women, but they have been rising since the early 1970s (table 1.3). Nevertheless, the increase among women may contain clues to some puzzling aspects of the growth of self-employment.

Characteristics of the Nonfarm Self-Employed

The self-employed differ from wage and salary workers in a number of respects. This section presents the social, demographic, and economic differences between these groups. It will be seen that, in broad terms, the long-term changes have affected the social and demographic more than the economic characteristics of nonfarm self-employment.

Gender

Although the data show that self-employment continues to grow among women, their self-employment rate continues to be below that of men (Becker 1984; Evans and Leighton 1987). Internal Revenue Service estimates of the growth of sole proprietorships for the period 1980–85 show that the number of enterprises owned by men increased by 31 percent while the number owned by women increased by 47 percent. Still, the number of proprietorships owned by men was nearly three times larger than the number owned by women (U.S. Small Business Administration [hereafter SBA] 1988). The recent growth in the number of self-employed women, however, has narrowed the gap.

Table 1.3, which is based on Social Security employment estimates, indexes the increase in the self-employment rates of men and women. The rate for men has tended to remain relatively flat, while the rate for women has risen steadily from about one-third to one-half the rate for men. Recent CPS data suggest, however, that the rate for women may have flattened at just below 6 percent of the total nonfarm employment rate for women (Department of Labor 1988, *Labor Force Statistics*).

Age

All studies of self-employment have remarked that the self-employed are generally substantially older than their counterparts in wage and salary employment. None of the studies, however, has tracked the changes in age distribution for the period before the increase in self-employment or for the period following. Social Security data, again, permit such tracking by gender as well as time (table 1.4). The data confirm that throughout the post–World War II period self-employed workers of both sexes have continued to be older than wage and salary workers; that until the mid-1970s there was little change in the age gap between the two classes of workers; and, rather surprisingly, that until the marked increase in the participation of women in self-employment, the age of self-employed women exceeded by a substantial margin that of men. The narrowing of the age difference between self-employed and other women after 1975 was probably the result of a cohort effect wherein recently self-employed women were younger and more numerous than women who had entered self-employment in earlier years.

Self-employment among nonfarm workers is clearly a mid–work life phenomenon for most men and women. In their study of the determinants

TABLE 1.4. MEDIAN AGES OF WORKERS, BY SEX AND TYPE OF EM-
PLOYMENT, SELECTED YEARS, 1955–1986

	Male			Female		
Year	All workers	Self-employed	Differential	All workers	Self-employed	Differential
1955	38	46	8	36	51	15
1960	38	48	10	38	51	13
1965	38	48	10	38	52	14
1970	37	48	11	35	52	17
1975	34	47	13	32	48	16
1980	33	44	11	32	42	10
1982	33	44	11	33	42	9
1984	34	43	9	33	41	8
1986	33	43	10	32	41	9

SOURCE: U.S. Department of Health and Human Services, Social Security Administration, *Social Security Bulletin, Annual Statistical Supplement, 1988.*

of self-employment in a life cycle framework, Evans and Leighton (1989) show that the propensity among white males to be self-employed increased with age, rising from slightly over 2 percent for workers twenty-one to twenty-five years of age to nearly 9 percent for workers fifty-six to sixty. Nevertheless, in their regression analysis of the probability of switching from wage and salary to self-employment, age did not prove to be a significant predictor. Likewise, Blau (1987), in a time-series analysis of the recent rise in nonfarm self-employment, did not find age to be a statistically significant independent variable. The long-term relative constancy of the age difference between the self-employed and wage and salary workers and the findings of these two studies strongly indicate that age may be a proxy for other determinants, including some that may be subjective or statistically unobservable, rather than a determinant in itself. Individual and family asset accumulation or changes in work attitudes over the course of the work life cycle are two such possibilities.

EDUCATION

It is often assumed that education increases the probability that someone will be self-employed, possibly because the entrepreneur may find a higher rate of return on his or her educational investment when self-employed than could be obtained as an employee. Evans and Leighton (1989) tested this hypothesis with grouped CPS data for the period 1967–85 on white men and women. Considering unincorporated self-employed only, they found a weak positive association between levels of educational attainment for men but a strong association for women. In a further analysis of entry into self-employment for men under the age of forty, as might be expected, education increased the likelihood of self-employment at a specific point in time but had little effect over time on a given population cohort.

Current Population Survey data for May 1983, comparing full-time unincorporated self-employed with full-time wage and salary workers, show that a higher proportion of the self-employed have four or more years of college and that a smaller proportion have a high school or less than a high school education (SBA, *State of Small Business, 1986*). Fragmentary data for the 1970s, however, suggest a small difference in educational attainment favoring wage and salary workers. The recent shift in favor of the self-employed may have occurred in part because of a higher rate of retirement or death among the older, less educated cohorts of the self-employed or because newer entrants to self-employment have higher educational attainment levels.

RACIAL STATUS

Self-employment and small business have long served as a vehicle by which various ethnic, religious, and racial groups have entered the mainstream economy and achieved upward economic and social mobility, if not for themselves then for their children and grandchildren. For some groups, particularly among recent immigrants, self-employment still serves that function. Self-employment rates among ethnic and racial minorities are substantially below the overall rate, however. A persistently low rate among black workers is the major contributor to this observation. Data from the 1980 Census of Population (table 1.5) show that self-employment rates for black workers are about one-third of the all-group rate. By contrast, rates for Asian-Americans, are closer to the all-group rate.

As Evans and Leighton (1987) remark, the drastically lower self-employment rate among blacks is a "puzzle." Their own study, for instance, finds no trend for the period 1967–85, whereas Becker (1984) reports a decline for blacks from 5.5 to 3.8 percent of total self-employment. Other reports indicate growth in self-employment and small business ownership among blacks in excess of overall employment growth. One such report indicates that the rate of increase in self-employment among blacks after

TABLE 1.5. PERCENTAGE SELF-EMPLOYED, BY GENDER AND RACE, 1980[a]

	Both	Male	Female
All groups	6.8	9.2	3.4
Black	2.4	3.5	1.2
Hispanic	3.8	4.9	2.1
Asian	6.2	8.2	4.0

SOURCE: U.S. Bureau of the Census 1984a.
[a]Includes agriculture.

the 1981–82 recession was twice that of the recession period (SBA, *State of Small Business, 1986*). This important issue will be discussed further in chapter 4.

INDUSTRIAL DISTRIBUTION AND TRENDS

Both wage and salary workers and the nonfarm self-employed were engaged predominantly in the service sector in 1987 (table 1.6). The principal difference was their respective shares of personal and business services. The self-employed have by far the larger relative number in that subsector but account for only one-tenth of total nonfarm employment in those industries.

Because nonfarm self-employment over the years has been predominantly located in the service sector, it has been less markedly affected by the overall shift of employment toward that sector. Estimates of industrial distribution by Lebergott (1964) show that about three-quarters of nonfarm self-employment in the pre–World War I period was in service sector industries. By 1987 that fraction was only slightly greater (table 1.6). Over the past eighty years the growth of the service sector as a whole, and of the nonfarm economy in general, has been at the expense of manufacturing. Among the service industries, however, there have been significant changes in the relative shares of self-employment. Data from both the IRS on sole proprietorships and the BLS household survey confirm that the highest rates of self-employment growth between the late 1950s and the early 1980s were in finance, insurance, and real estate and in personal and business services. By contrast, transportation and communication and trade grew at considerably less than half the average rate of growth for all industries during that period. Indeed, retail trade, traditionally the site of significant opportunity for small business ownership, suffered a decline.

TABLE 1.6. PERCENTAGE DISTRIBUTION OF NONFARM EMPLOYMENT, BY INDUSTRY AND CLASS OF WORKER, 1987

Industry	Private wage and salary	Self-employed No.	Self-employed % total nonfarm
All industries (in thousands)	83,970	8,201	9.8
Mining	0.9	0.3	3.3
Construction	6.5	16.8	18.6
Manufacturing	24.3	4.3	1.7
Transportation and communication	7.1	4.1	4.3
Retail trade	25.4	22.4	7.9
Finance, insurance, real estate	8.3	7.3	7.7
Personal and business services	27.4	44.7	10.2

SOURCE: U.S. Department of Labor, *Employment and Earnings, 1988.*

The industrial distribution of nonfarm self-employment is distinctly different for men and women, with the latter more heavily involved in personal and business services while the former are more likely to be found in construction and manufacturing. More attention will be given to this matter in chapter 4.

OCCUPATIONAL DISTRIBUTION AND TRENDS

The occupational patterns of employment differentiate the self-employed from wage and salary workers even more than do their respective industrial distributions. For both types of employment, again, there are marked gender differences despite similar occupational trends. Table 1.7 provides an overview of the occupational distributions by type of employment and gender for the period 1950–80.

Data for the broad occupational groups show the degree to which the occupational paths of the self-employed and wage and salary workers have diverged. The differences are particularly marked in the so-called white-collar occupations and the skilled crafts. In the professional and technical occupations, men and women in wage and salary jobs and the self-employed increased their shares by similar magnitudes. In the nonfarm managerial group, however, employment shares remained relatively stable in wage and salary employment but declined drastically for the self-employed.

The most marked change for the self-employed in the manual and service occupations took place in the skilled crafts, in which women increased their

TABLE 1.7. OCCUPATIONAL DISTRIBUTION OF NONFARM EMPLOYMENT, BY CLASS OF WORKER[a] AND GENDER, 1950 AND 1980[b] (in percent)

Occupation	Male 1950		Male 1980[c]		Female 1950		Female 1980[c]	
	Total	Self-employed	Total	Self-employed	Total	Self-employed	Total	Self-employed
All occupations (in thousands)	33,900	4,320	53,597	3,984	15,154	845	41,231	1,401
Professional and technical	8.6	12.2	14.5	19.9	12.8	12.1	18.2	19.2
Nonfarm managers and proprietors	12.4	49.7	13.2	14.9	4.4	38.5	7.4	12.9
Sales	7.6	7.4	9.5	20.0	8.7	11.8	11.3	24.4
Clerical	7.6	0.5	10.0	0.9	28.2	5.7	32.0	8.9
Craft and kindred	22.3	16.5	21.7	29.6	1.6	1.8	2.4	4.6
Operatives	23.7	6.9	17.7	8.5	19.9	8.2	9.7	3.1
Nonfarm labor	9.6	2.5	6.5	1.2	0.8	0.3	2.1	0.6
Personal service, except private household	6.9	3.8	7.2	_d	12.6	17.8	16.3	26.3
Private household	0.2	_d	_d	_d	_d	_d	_d	_d

SOURCES: U.S. Bureau of the Census 1950 and 1980.

[a]Excludes employees of own corporation.

[b]1960 and 1970 omitted in order to highlight gender differences.

[c]While the numbers for total nonfarm employment appear to be correct for both years, the estimates for self-employment in 1980 are inconsistent with data from other sources. Current Population Report estimates for April 1980, the census month, show 4,727,000 male and 2,018,000 female nonfarm self-employed (U.S. Department of Labor, Employment and Earnings, 1980).

[d]Less than 0.1 percent.

TABLE 1.8. PERCENTAGE SELF-EMPLOYED, BY GENDER, SELECTED OCCUPATIONS, 1980

Occupation	Male	Female
All occupations	9.2	3.7
Managerial and professional	10.3	4.8
All professions	12.2	4.3
Architects	30.0	20.7
Health diagnosing	40.6	20.0
Lawyers and judges	42.4	14.9
Technical, sales, and administrative support	8.2	2.5
Sales	15.6	7.3
Service occupations	3.8	5.0
Personal services	24.9	22.3
Skilled trades	10.2	6.7
Construction trades	17.5	15.9
Precision textile and apparel	27.1	21.2

SOURCE: U.S. Bureau of the Census 1984c.

share of self-employment by 155 percent and men by almost 80 percent. The shares of wage and salary employment in these occupations, by contrast, remained more or less constant. All women made large relative gains in nonhousehold personal and business services, but the gains of self-employed women exceeded those of female wage and salary workers by almost 50 percent. More recent data, however, based on a different scheme of occupational classification, show little change in the occupational distributions of the self-employed compared with wage and salary workers. The nonfarm self-employed are proportionately more numerous in executive and managerial, professional, marketing and sales, and precision craft occupations, while wage and salary workers are more often found in technical and administrative support and semiskilled and unskilled jobs.[3]

Despite their increased participation in self-employment in the postwar period, women have not yet achieved occupational parity with self-employed men (table 1.8). Even in those occupations with a long tradition of independent practice, such as medicine, law, and architecture, self-employment among women is on average only about one-third that of men. Somewhat surprising, however, are the relatively high rates for women in the construction and apparel industries.

---

3. Based on calculations from data in Silvestri and Lukesiewicz (1989).

EARNINGS

Compared with wage and salary workers, the nonfarm self-employed appear to earn less. As in any earnings comparison, the degree and direction of divergence depends on a number of varying characteristics and circumstances, among them gender, age, occupation, and period of observation. Evans and Leighton (1987) report that for the period 1976–85 wage and salary workers on average enjoyed only a slight advantage over the self-employed—$22,832 per year versus $21,851. But Becker (1984) reports that in 1982 annual earnings in self-employment were only 70 percent of earnings in wage employment. Such estimates, however, conceal significant statistical variations, such as those due to gender differences, the effect of incorporation, and whether there were single or multiple sources of income. In chapter 3, devoted to earnings comparisons, I will discuss the view that the apparently unfavorable earnings position of the self-employed is a relatively recent development, representing an inversion of an earlier relationship.

HOURS WORKED

Differences in earnings, of course, often depend substantially on differences in the amount of labor supplied. Bureau of Labor Statistics data show that in 1985 the nonfarm self-employed worked an average of 48.3 hours weekly compared with 42.8 hours for full-time wage workers (U.S. Department of Labor, *Employment and Earnings, 1986*). This difference is substantially smaller than in earlier years. Becker (1984) reported a greater decline for the period 1979–83 in average weekly hours worked for all nonfarm self-employed than for nonfarm wage workers: a fourfold difference, from two hours per week for the former to thirty minutes for the latter.

The proportion of full-time workers among the self-employed exceeds the proportion among wage workers by a large fraction. In 1985, for example, 76 percent of the nonfarm self-employed worked full time compared with 56 percent of wage workers. Part-time employment for economic, that is, involuntary, reasons, however, was higher among the self-employed that year: 7.5 percent compared with 5.5 percent of wage workers. But even given such differences, it appears that with respect to time worked nonfarm self-employed and wage workers are more alike today than in earlier periods.

The proportion of nonfarm self-employed working a full fifty- to fifty-two-week year exceeds the fraction who do so among wage and salary workers, though the difference has narrowed over time. By 1978 the gap had narrowed to less than 2 percent, mainly because of a decline in the number of self-employed working full-year jobs. The relatively higher rate of growth of part-time work among the self-employed may have contributed to the convergence with wage workers in both hours worked per week and weeks worked per year. Between May 1979 and May 1983, part-time unincorporated self-employment increased by 19.2 percent, while part-time employment among wage and salary workers increased by only 4.5 percent (SBA, *State of Small Business, 1986*).

Despite the dramatic postwar increase in multiple wage-earner families, there has been no noticeable increase, at least until 1980, in the proportion of individuals holding two or more jobs concurrently. The proportion of workers holding multiple jobs has not increased among wage and salary workers or among the self-employed in the nonfarm sectors. There has, however, been a change in the role of self-employment. Self-employment as the primary job declined between 1955 and 1980 but has shown a steady rise as the secondary job, consistent with the rise of part-time self-employment. In 1955, self-employment constituted about 13 percent of second jobs; by 1980, 25 percent of these jobs were in self-employment. It is likely that the increase in self-employment among women is important in this development, but published data on workers who hold multiple jobs do not provide the breakdown necessary to confirm this hypothesis.

EMPLOYMENT STABILITY

Although it seems paradoxical, self-employment is far from a perfect defense against unemployment.[4] An annual average rate of unemployment among experienced nonfarm self-employed workers calculated for the 1950–81 period (U.S. Department of Labor, *Employment and Earnings,* various issues) was 1.6 percent compared with about 6 percent for the labor force as a whole. Data on business failure rates and on rates of transition to and from self-employment, though far from complete, suggest the employment risks involved. The 1987 *State of Small Business* indicates that in the previous year there were 241,870 business starts, of which about 80 percent were small businesses (i.e., firms with fewer then five hundred employees). Business failures in 1986 were reported to be 62,300, or about 25 percent of business starts. A study cited in the report, moreover, suggests that the failure rate

---

4. Indeed, as later discussion will indicate, self-employment may in some cases be a form of so-called disguised unemployment.

may be understated by as much as a factor of ten, in that the Dun and Bradstreet records on which these data are based report only enterprises that have been rated for credit. Since many small businesses, especially those characterized by self-employment, use personal or informal sources of finance, their history escapes the Dun and Bradstreet recording system.

In the most comprehensive effort to date to understand the reemergence of self-employment, Evans and Leighton (1989) analyzed the turnover experience of self-employed male workers from 1966–67 to 1978–80. Although those entering self-employment exceeded those leaving in each year of the period, the authors found that 50 to 60 percent of the entrants, on average, "failed" during the first two to three years after entry and returned to wage employment or unemployment or left the labor force entirely. A British study of the self-employed reports that in 1987–88, 23 percent of those persons who had been self-employed one year earlier were unemployed and another 27 percent had left the labor force (Hakim 1989).

Developments Abroad

The basic patterns of nonfarm self-employment in other industrialized countries are similar to those in the United States. There are differences in levels across countries, but only a few countries have experienced a strong increase in the relative importance of self-employment. Among the few experiencing growth, the United Kingdom stands out, with an increase of nearly 50 percent in nonfarm self-employment in the 1981–88 period (Hakim 1989). Despite the growth in the United States and the United Kingdom, Elfring's data for 1960 and 1984 show an overall decline in the rate of self-employment for seven countries, from 22 to 13 percent (Elfring 1988).[5] These estimates include agriculture, however, and exclude the upturn in nonfarm self-employment in some countries during the 1970s. Table 1.9 shows the levels of nonfarm self-employment for the member countries of the European Economic Community (EEC) in 1984.

During the previous twenty years, only a few countries experienced a definite upward trend in nonfarm self-employment, among them Canada, Australia, and the United Kingdom. In most other industrialized countries the relative importance of self-employment, as well as its industrial distribution, remained relatively unchanged.[6] As in the United States, self-

---

5. France, Germany, Japan, Netherlands, Sweden, United Kingdom, and the United States.

6. The findings of a recent report by the International Labour Office, though covering a broader range of countries, including the lesser-developed and the centrally planned countries, are consistent with these observations for the industrialized market economies (ILO 1990).

TABLE 1.9. PERCENTAGE DISTRIBUTION OF NONFARM SELF-EMPLOYMENT IN EEC, BY SECTOR, 1984 (in thousands)

Country	Total nonfarm employment	% Self-employed		
		All sectors	Industry	Services
Federal Republic of Germany	24,677	7.8	2.0	5.8
France	19,420	9.1	2.6	6.5
Italy	17,933	21.3	5.6	15.7
Netherlands	4,709	8.6	1.3	7.3
Belgium	3,338	14.0	2.5	11.5
Luxembourg	138	7.9	1.4	6.5
United Kingdom	31,317	7.5	2.4	5.1
Ireland	912	11.4	3.3	8.1
Denmark	2,299	7.5	2.0	5.5
Greece	2,471	26.5	8.3	19.0

SOURCE: Statistical Office of the European Communities 1986.

employment is predominantly located in the service industries for both men and women (table 1.10). Elfring's analysis of trends in service sector employment in seven of the ten countries in the Organization for Economic Cooperation and Development (OECD) shows that in all but one case, the United Kingdom, the share of self-employment declined, from 17 to 11 percent, during the 1960–84 period (1988). Other industrial sectors apparently have accounted for the increase in self-employment in some countries. Burgess (1988) indicates that in Australia the rise has been in manufacturing, finance and real estate, and community services.

As in the United States, the participation of women in self-employment is well below that of men (table 1.11), though women account for a significant and, in most of the countries, an increasing fraction of nonfarm self-employment. Burgess (1988) indicates an increase in self-employment among women in Australia, from 22 percent in 1973 to 30 percent in 1986. Carter and Cannon (1988) report that between 1981 and 1987, the number of self-employed women in Great Britain increased by 70 percent, while the increase among men was barely 30 percent. They also report that in Sweden and Finland fully one-fourth of owner-managers are women.

As suggested, self-employment patterns, such as the industrial distribution, differ sharply among countries. For example, in 1983, nonfarm self-employment in the goods sectors of the EEC countries ranged from 4 percent in the Netherlands to 15 percent in Italy and 24 percent in Greece,

TABLE 1.10.   PERCENTAGE OF NONFARM SELF-EMPLOYMENT IN SER-
VICES IN EEC, BY GENDER, 1983

Country	Male	Female
EEC	66	87
Federal Republic of Germany	79	88
France	64	91
Italy	68	83
Netherlands	80	92
Belgium	75	95
United Kingdom	61	90
Denmark	67	91
Greece	65	76

SOURCE: Statistical Office of the European Communities 1986.

TABLE 1.11.   SELF-EMPLOYED AS PERCENTAGE OF WOMEN IN NON-
FARM EMPLOYMENT, SELECTED COUNTRIES, 1963–1983

Country	1963	1967	1971	1975	1979	1983
Australia	20.5[a]	27.0	26.7	28.4	29.1	30.8
Belgium	30.5	30.5	27.9	27.8	27.3	27.8
Canada	N.A.	30.6	31.9	30.6	35.3	37.4
Federal Republic of Germany	23.7	22.1	22.5	22.5	23.0	23.4
Italy	30.3	27.6	27.5	27.3	20.8	N.A.
Japan	36.3	36.9	34.1	32.2	34.3	36.6
Spain	N.A.	N.A.	23.4	25.4	22.9	24.3
Sweden	N.A.	N.A.	19.6	21.4	25.4	28.9
United Kingdom	23.3	23.6	21.5	20.7	19.3	25.2
United States	N.A.	25.2	25.2	26.0	29.2	32.3

SOURCE: Organization for Economic Cooperation and Development 1985.
[a]1964.

whereas self-employment in the goods sectors of the EEC countries as a
whole was only about 8 percent.[7] Data on time worked is scanty for European countries. In the EEC countries in 1983, the pattern appears similar to
that of the United States, with a higher incidence of part-time work among
wage and salary workers. In that year, which may not be typical, 8 percent

7. For a detailed industrial breakdown of self-employment for three periods, the early
1960s, 1973, and 1984, see Elfring 1988, appendix D.

of self-employment was part time, compared with 12 percent of wage and salary work. Unlike the pattern in the United States, however, the incidence of part-time work among self-employed women in the EEC countries was proportionately lower than among wage and salary workers. Women in those countries accounted for 85 percent of part-time employment overall but for only 60 percent of part-time self-employment.

As is common nearly everywhere, detailed occupational data by type of employment are unavailable in published form. Limited evidence for one country, Germany, indicates that in 1982 self-employment was located in foreign and domestic trade occupations and in professional and business services. Seventy-five percent of self-employed men and 95 percent of self-employed women were in such occupations (Statistisches Bundesamt 1982). The pattern in the United Kingdom for men in 1971 was much like that of the United States, with the heaviest concentrations of self-employed workers in construction and allied trades, sales, and business and professional services (Scase and Goffee 1982). The current distribution by gender is similar. In 1988, 85 percent of self-employed women were engaged in services, while only 54 percent of self-employed men were in that sector *(Employment Gazette* 1989).

It would be interesting to speculate on the factors underlying the differences among these countries in the levels of self-employment and the participation of women. Unfortunately, the data sources represented in tables 1.9, 1.10, and 1.11 allow for little speculation. There is the suggestion that nonfarm self-employment may be inversely related to the level of industrial development, as in the cases of Italy and Greece, but Denmark appears to be a counterexample. Similarly, there does not appear to be a consistent relationship between market size, as represented by population, and the levels of self-employment, assuming that small enterprises are more likely where the potential for economies of scale are limited.

Summary and Conclusions

Following a long-term decline in both absolute and relative terms, nonfarm self-employment appears to have reestablished itself as a growing and potentially significant component of the American economy. The upturn appears to have begun in the early 1970s and has continued steadily for approximately a decade, although there are some recent signs of a slower rate of development. In broad industrial and occupational terms, the turn-around has not been accompanied by marked shifts; however, recent studies suggest major structural changes within those sectors, notably in services.

The review of the data shows that, on average, the self-employed differ from wage and salary workers in their personal and social characteristics. But except in one very important respect—the percentage of women represented—these characteristics have not changed markedly during the post–World War II period. Compared with wage and salary workers, the self-employed are older and more likely to be men and may have less—but not substantially less—formal education. Blacks, relative to their numbers in the labor force, are very much underrepresented in nonfarm self-employment, while some recent immigrant groups, notably Asians, have achieved rates of self-employment almost equal to those of the native-born white population. The full-time self-employed, despite some reduction in weekly hours worked, still tend to work longer hours and more weeks of the year than their wage and salary counterparts.

Although the proportion of self-employed women remains substantially lower than that of self-employed men, women have been a major contributor to the recent growth of self-employment both here and abroad. It is possible that this development, which has escaped notice in recent studies, may provide clues to some of the issues that will be addressed in later chapters. These include questions about the timing of the reemergence of nonfarm self-employment. Why, for instance, has the growth of self-employment occurred in the face of falling earnings? Has there been a significant change in the motivation for becoming self-employed? That is, is self-employment driven more by the absence or disappearance of more attractive alternatives than by positive values?

CHAPTER TWO

Determinants of
Self-Employment

Although still modest, interest in nonfarm self-employment as a social and labor market phenomenon has grown with self-employment itself. Until recently, most of the literature has been micro-oriented, focused primarily on self-employment as a personal choice dictated for the most part by demographic, social, and cultural characteristics. Broader developments in the economy, especially in the labor market, have played no explanatory role in the majority of studies. Within the past several years, however, a few studies explicitly directed toward understanding the reemergence of self-employment have introduced structural and environmental factors into their accounts. Some studies have discussed these broader factors theoretically, while others have tested them empirically. Regardless, thus far the overall result falls short of a satisfactory accounting. In particular, questions about the timing of the upturn in nonfarm self-employment and its growth in the face of not only relatively lower but falling earnings by comparison with wage and salary workers still lack acceptable answers.

In this chapter, the literature is reviewed from both micro and macro perspectives in a search for the explanation of the revival of self-employment. In addition to the findings of various studies, I discuss the influence of factors absent from the macro-oriented literature.

The Self-Employment Decision

With a few exceptions, the question of who becomes self-employed and why they do so has received little attention in the contemporary literature of economics. At an earlier time, as Evans and Leighton (1987) make clear in their review of theories of entrepreneurship, there was vigorous theoretical discussion by economists of the characteristics and motivations of those assuming an entrepreneurial role (Knight 1933; Schumpeter 1934). Recent discussion of this question has been sparse and largely theoretical, divided in general by two different sets of assumptions. One theory regards entrepreneurs as individuals with particular abilities. According to this theory, self-knowledge of these abilities motivates individuals to establish their own enterprises, usually as self-employed persons.[1] The contrasting view assumes that self-employment is largely opportunistic. The self-employed are not endowed with special abilities that differentiate them from individuals in wage and salary jobs but instead are merely responding to the environmental circumstances in which they find themselves in a particular place or at a particular time.[2]

There is no obvious way to decide a priori the validity of either of these approaches. In the remainder of this section, then, the focus is on the results of studies that have attempted to test empirically the relationships between personal and social characteristics and the likelihood of becoming self-employed.[3]

In the previous chapter I noted that, in contrast to wage and salary workers, the self-employed are generally older, slightly less educated, and less likely to be female or a member of a principal ethnic or racial minority. With the exceptions noted in the following discussion, most studies have simply recorded such differences rather than examined them as possible explanations for why someone chooses to be self-employed. At issue is whether these differentiating characteristics, in and of themselves, help determine the level and rate of nonfarm self-employment. For example, since the self-employed tend to be older, is there a relationship between the aging

---

1. For a contemporary exposition of this view, see Casson (1982), who argues that neoclassical economists can never understand the entrepreneurial role as long as it assumes decision making in the firm to be impersonal and unaffected by social, psychological, or cultural influences. Blau (1985) also takes this approach, though he deals with self-employment as an outcome of rural-urban movement in a lesser-developed economy.

2. Burgess (1988) and Evans and Leighton (1989) provide examples of this approach, though they include some variables in their model that might be construed as belonging to the generic viewpoint. For an earlier exposition and empirical study representing the opportunistic hypothesis, see Oxenfeldt (1943).

3. Both the theoretical literature and a number of empirical studies assume an identity between entrepreneurship and self-employment. In my view, the two are conceptually distinct but have been muddied by the lack of measures that would distinguish those who innovate from those offering labor directly rather than through an intermediary, such as an employer.

of the population and, consequently, the labor force and the increase in the rate of self-employment, other things being equal?

AGE

All studies appear to show a consistently positive relationship between age and the rate of self-employment. Nonfarm self-employment is rarely an entry occupation into the labor force, with the exception of some professional occupations and the casual employment of teenagers. For the labor force as a whole and for cohorts of white males under the age of forty, however, Evans and Leighton (1989) found that for a pooled sample of white males drawn from the Current Population Survey for the period 1968–87, the likelihood of entering self-employment from wage work in any given year was independent of age. After the age of twenty-five to thirty, annual entry rates for this sample varied within a narrow 2 to 3 percent range. The increase in the rate of self-employment during that period occurred because exit rates fell below entry rates in the 1970s. Although Brock, Evans, and Phillips (1986) found age to be a statistically significant and positive influence on the likelihood of self-employment among full-time employed males,[4] they also reported that this effect tended to decline with advancing years. Iams's study of Social Security sample data (1987) also found that the relationship between age and self-employment tended to stabilize, though in that case among workers in their late forties.

Earlier studies of retirement behavior by Fuchs (1982) and Quinn (1980), although dealing with somewhat different demographic groups, are similar in their findings on the age–self-employment relationship. Fuchs found there was very little difference between early and later cohorts of urban white males in the age–self-employment relationship, indicating a high degree of stability in the work patterns of both wage and salary workers and the self-employed. In that study and in Quinn's, stabilization of the relationship occurs mainly because self-employed males withdraw from the labor force more slowly than their wage and salary counterparts, many of whom may be subject to mandatory retirement. The most recent study of the postretirement experience of Social Security beneficiaries (Iams 1987) confirms this result, finding that the relatively higher rates of self-employment among working beneficiaries are largely accounted for by in-

---

4. They excluded professional workers, farmers, and workers over age sixty-five from the sample.

dividuals who were already self-employed at the time of retirement, rather than by a marked increase in self-employment among individuals who were wage earners at the time they retired.[5] The conclusion seems to be that the age–self-employment relationship is a demographic rather than a behavioral phenomenon.

Age is probably a proxy for other factors that may govern entry into self-employment. In fact, Fuchs (1982) reported that age and the switch from wage and salary jobs to self-employment were not in themselves statistically significant. A variety of positive and negative factors that may be age-related could account for the relatively higher rates of self-employment among older workers, however. Wage and salary workers in various manual employment may suffer a loss of physical stamina with age, while self-employed workers can often control the amount and pace of work. Poorer health with advancing age is another reason for becoming self-employed. Technical or skill obsolescence, a concomitant of aging in some occupations, may lead to self-employment in activities requiring less advanced knowledge and skill. Mandatory retirement simply because of age also pushes people into self-employment. Fuchs (1982) found such policies to be statistically significant for men who switched from wage jobs to self-employment.

The positive reasons for entering self-employment at a later age involve two principal factors. First, time is needed to build the human capital (i.e., skill and experience) and the means (i.e., personal savings) required to establish one's own business. Although they found no statistically significant relationship between total labor market experience and self-employment in their longitudinal analysis, Evans and Leighton (1989) report that in their study the men with greater family net worth were more likely to become self-employed. In their cross-sectional analysis for 1981, however, time in the labor force had a strong positive influence on the probability that white males would become self-employed. Second, as a function of age-related time in the labor market, the development of one's reputation and goodwill may be essential for the survival of one's own future business. Professional and managerial workers who establish their own businesses frequently appear to do so with the expectation that their previous clientele will follow in sufficient numbers to make their start-up feasible.

---

5. Retirement behavior, though not considered by their study, may partly explain the stabilization of self-employment rates among older men reported in Evans and Leighton 1989.

GENDER AND RACE

A curious fact about studies of self-employment, including those examining its recent growth, is the relative neglect of the role of women. I shall devote portions of chapters 3 and 4 to this subject; it is worth reporting here, however, that beyond noting gender differences in self-employment rates, no studies have examined the dominant role of women in the revitalization of self-employment. The analysis either makes no distinction between rates for men and women (Leveson 1968; Blau 1987) or excludes women when testing propositions about entry into self-employment (Fuchs 1980; Brock, Evans, and Phillips 1986). Although Evans and Leighton (1987) analyzed the determinants of entry separately for white men and white women, they did not attempt to explain why the self-employment rate among women has grown relative to that of men. This neglect is curious in that the marked increase in labor force participation among women has been the major overall labor market development of the post–World War II period and the focus of much labor market theory and analysis. The patterns and problems of women in small business, for instance, have been a regular feature of the Small Business Administration's annual reports,[6] which contain much interesting data, possibly the best on this subject. Neither the development itself nor the availability of data, however, has as yet inspired research on the overall influence of the increase of women in nonfarm self-employment.

By contrast, the relatively low participation of ethnic and racial minorities in nonfarm self-employment has been the subject of some research. There are data on minority businesses, thanks mainly to the efforts of the SBA and a few other statistical sources. Again, the subject is of sufficient interest to deserve more extended treatment in a later chapter. Here it can only be remarked that the experience of minorities contrasts sharply with that of women, especially in the case of blacks. In chapter 4, I will examine possible reasons blacks have not utilized self-employment as a vehicle for upward economic and social mobility.

EDUCATION AND OCCUPATION

Because they are closely related to people's choices of jobs and careers, education and occupation are treated together. One might hypothesize that with the general rise in the level of education, especially among younger

---

6. These reports, which began during the Reagan administration in 1981, are contained in *The State of Small Business: A Report of the President.* The SBA report itself is mandated by the Business Economic Policy Act of 1980.

population cohorts, and the concomitant growth of the professional and white-collar occupations, self-employment would increase, other factors held constant. Educational investments in human capital might have a higher net yield if self-employment could protect that investment from exploitation, as implied by Wolpin (1977) in his discussion of screening and education. A few studies seem to bear out this hypothesis. Brock, Evans, and Phillips (1986), for example, reported that college graduates were more likely to become self-employed whereas high school dropouts were less likely to and that age in combination with education had a positive effect on the probability of becoming self-employed. Evans and Leighton (1989) obtained conflicting results, depending on their data source. Although their cohort analysis of males in the National Longitudinal Survey panel and their analysis of pooled CPS data showed that high school dropouts were less likely to enter self-employment, the two sources diverged on the significance of educational achievement. Number of years of education was not statistically significant in the cohort analysis but was significant for the CPS data, in which college graduates and postgraduates were strongly inclined toward self-employment.

Self-employment rates historically have been highest among professional and managerial occupations. Although few studies have included occupation as a dimension of self-employment, those studies that have confirm this generalization (Brock, Evans, and Phillips 1986; Evans and Leighton 1989). Similarly, Form (1985), confining his study of the self-employed to manual workers, reported that skilled crafts workers were more likely than other manual workers to be self-employed.

One must view these results on occupational differences somewhat skeptically for at least three reasons. First, none of the studies has examined gender differences. Second, in the few studies that have paid attention to occupation, the categories were so broad as virtually to defy meaningful interpretation. Third, the long-term trend among the traditional professions, as will be shown in chapter 4, has been toward wage and salary rather than independent employment. Women in managerial and professional occupations have contributed to this development because of their lower self-employment rates. They are by no means the sole contributor, however.

NONPECUNIARY MOTIVATION

The foregoing review of factors contributing to or inhibiting entry into self-employment has drawn attention to the characteristics of the self-employed. The question of why individuals who are not obviously different from wage and salary workers become self-employed remains to be explored. If the data on earnings differences discussed in chapter 3 are valid, monetary advantage has not been a dominant reason, at least during the recent period of growth.

The literature discussing the reasons individuals turn to self-employment draws largely on theories of entrepreneurship and generally lacks empirical content. Moreover, there appears to be a sharp division over whether the choice of self-employment is a rational act. Some earlier writers (Oxenfeldt 1943; Phillips, 1962) have taken the position that the self-employed are behaving irrationally, perhaps because they lack adequate information about market opportunities and risk or have been forced into self-employment by unemployment or adverse personal circumstances such as ill health and disability. More recent literature, perhaps reflecting the increase in the rate of self-employment, has generally adopted a more positive perspective, emphasizing such nonpecuniary advantages as greater control over the performance and use of one's work, greater flexibility in the use of time, the absence of institutional restraints, and so on.[7]

Tracking nonpecuniary reasons for self-employment, however, is an exercise in futility. Measuring attitudes and values is often observationally fugitive, even where sample sizes are adequate and representative. Moreover, in all empirical studies motivation is inferred after the decision to enter self-employment has been made. The workers surveyed thus differ from the theoretical ideal, that is, individuals contemplating the alternatives of continuing in wage employment or striking out on their own.

Efforts to measure motivation empirically have drawn on two related hypotheses. The more common of the two is virtually equivalent to the definition of self-employment, namely, that individuals with a strong sense of autonomy are more likely than others to be drawn toward self-employment. Casson (1982), for example, in his critique of the approach of neoclassical economics to entrepreneurship, hypothesizes that the entrepreneur has a perception that he or she is uniquely right for entrepreneurial enterprise and hopes on this account to profit from that perception.[8] The second hypothesis asserts that the self-employed are motivated by the desire for higher levels of job satisfaction.

---

7. See Casson (1982) and Burgess (1988). While these authors recognize that costs and risks are also attendant on self-employment, they incline to a more optimistic viewpoint.

8. In behavioral terms, Casson's entrepreneur does not seem to differ from the conventional "economic man," since in his discussion of the self-employment decision individuals are assumed to be comparing costs and benefits in real terms.

These ideas have been explored with and without wage and salary workers as the implicit control or comparison group. In a small case study of twenty-five sole proprietors and their spouses, Scase and Goffee (1982) found that while there was a latent desire for independence among their interviewees, most were forced into self-employment by redundancy or dissatisfaction with a wage job. Their interest was in making a living rather than in being autonomous.[9]

Eden (1975) compared wage and salary workers with the self-employed with respect to their career goals, degree of job satisfaction, and other sociopsychological aspects of their work. Although the self-employed registered comparatively higher levels of job satisfaction and control over work content, they paid a price in longer hours of work, greater emotional strain, more job instability, and greater income inequality. Controlling for age and gender differences between the two groups, Eden concluded that the virtues of self-employment were overrated, if not illusory.

Other recent studies, by contrast, have found some evidence to support the conventional wisdom. Fredland and Little (1985), in their study of middle-aged men, claim to have found evidence that the promise of psychic income is an important motivator in the choice of self-employment. This inference is based on the finding that there was no statistically significant difference between wage and salary earners and the self-employed with respect to human capital endowments; even though their money earnings were comparatively lower, the self-employed had a more positive attitude toward and greater commitment to their jobs than comparable wage and salary workers.

In his study of the same age-gender group, Daum (1984) reported a slightly higher degree of job satisfaction among the self-employed, but this factor appeared negligible in the transition from wage to self-employment. Evans and Leighton (1989) found that the men in their study who measured higher on a scale of internal control (presumably equivalent to their sense of independence) were more likely to be self-employed.

The issue of ascertaining whether there has been a marked change in workers' attitudes toward self-employment as a career alternative is problematic. There are as yet no indices that can measure such attitudes convincingly and that can be tracked over time with appropriate controls for other influences. Hakim (1989) studied a sample of persons in Great Britain

---

9. Most of the men in the sample had no interest in expanding their enterprises and employing others.

who were newly self-employed or who had recently ceased being self-employed. She concluded that, in comparison with the desire for greater independence, flexibility in dividing time between work and nonwork, financial gain, and unemployment were not primary motives for entering self-employment. Attitudes and work-related values prior to becoming self-employed were not canvassed, however.

At this point, entry into and retention in self-employment remains purely a behavioral phenomenon. There is a need for empirical research to distinguish those who enter self-employment with a strong sense of entrepreneurship from those who simply wish to sell their labor on the best terms available under the circumstances. Consideration of the structural and environmental factors that appear to influence changes in self-employment rates and composition may help us understand the behavioral aspect further.

Structural and Environmental Factors

Any sustained employment trend necessarily directs attention to variables that increase or decrease the opportunity for particular kinds of work. Some variables, though broad, may have strong effects on specific types of employment. Other variables may be more closely related to the phenomenon of interest. Two recent studies of the growth of nonfarm self-employment (Blau 1987 and Evans and Leighton 1987) have looked at both kinds of variables.[10] The following discussion of broad structural and environmental changes in the economy relies heavily on these studies.

Changes in aggregate demand would be expected to influence the timing of changes in employment and the distribution of workers between wage work and self-employment, depending on whether the change in demand was cyclical or secular. In either case, interindustry differences in demand are also likely to be important because of the differences in the distribution of the two types of employment, outlined in chapter 1.

The broadest measure of change in demand, the change in real gross national product (GNP), covering the period of interest suggests that growth of nonfarm self-employment was associated with a slowing of economic growth. Real GNP advanced at an annual rate of 3.5 percent in the 1950s and 4.6 percent in the 1960s but by only 3.2 percent in the 1970s when

---

10. Although Evans and Leighton's 1989 report overlaps substantially with their 1987 report, the more recent study is confined to the micro influences on the movement into and out of self-employment.

nonfarm self-employment experienced its highest postwar rate of increase (U.S. President 1988). Evans and Leighton (1987), the only researchers thus far to incorporate GNP as an explanatory variable, found the GNP to have a very small but statistically significant positive influence on rates of self-employment. For white males, a 10 percent increase in real GNP was accompanied by an increase of only 0.16 percent in the rate of self-employment for the unincorporated self-employed. The effect was even smaller and statistically insignificant among the incorporated self-employed. For women, the effect was significant only for incorporated entrepreneurs, producing a 0.75 percent increase in self-employment. This gender difference is probably associated with the difference in industrial and occupational distribution of self-employed men and women, discussed in chapter 4.

Another common measure of aggregate demand is the change in total employment derived from changes in national output and income. Aggregate nonfarm employment during the post–World War II period, when observed in five-year units, indicates a higher annual rate of growth from 1965 to 1969 than from 1970 to 1974, even though overall employment increased more rapidly in the late 1970s when the rate of increase in self-employment may have been slowing (U.S. Department of Labor 1985). In his effort to construct a historical series for nonfarm self-employment, Lebergott (1964) remarked that self-employment tended to follow the course of total nonfarm employment but lagged by as much as a year and a half. During the period of rapid growth of self-employment in the 1970s, however, the aggregate rate of civilian unemployment was higher than in the previous decade.[11]

EFFECT OF THE BUSINESS CYCLE

The vagaries of the relationship between measures of aggregate demand and the trend in self-employment outlined above invite examination of the literature on the cyclical aspects of self-employment. Have the changes in self-employment rates been primarily a response to alternations in the aggregate economy, in much the same way, say, as the rise of street-corner apple sellers in the 1930s was a response to that era's economic downfall? Ac-

---

11. During the 1960s, the unemployment rate for all workers averaged 4.6 percent of the civilian labor force. In the 1970s, the average unemployment rate was 6.1 percent (U.S. President 1988).

cording to this thesis, a fall in the rate of economic growth and rising unemployment leads to increased effort to create one's own job. The numbers of temporary or transient self-employed, distinguished by Quinn (1980) from the "career" self-employed, increase under these circumstances until opportunities to return to wage employment improve.

Several studies report findings in support of the belief that nonfarm self-employment is inversely related to business fluctuations. Ray (1975) and Becker (1984) both report evidence of countercyclical increases in self-employment during the post–World War II period. Becker, however, reported that the largest gains in self-employment were made in the recovery phase of the business cycle, again suggesting a lag in the self-employment response to recession. The Organization for Economic Cooperation and Development (1986), allowing for some differences in the definitions of nonfarm self-employment among thirteen countries, including the United States, estimated the sensitivity of self-employment to cyclical changes in civilian employment. The self-employment rate was found to be statistically significant at the 5 percent level and negatively related to a business cycle measure in eight of the countries and negative but not significant in two other countries. By contrast, in four countries—Austria, France, Sweden, and the United Kingdom—no cyclical sensitivity was found. Absolute changes in self-employment were more closely related to a secular time trend, negatively in two countries but positively in nine others. Highfield and Smiley (1986) and Bishop (1987) concluded that the rate of small business growth tends to increase during periods of sluggish economic growth. Neither of these studies, however, assigns major importance to business cycles.

A few studies of individual sectors and industries have investigated self-employment as a response to economic change, with inconclusive results. Fuchs's study (1968) of the service sector for the period 1947–65 found that compared with wage and salary workers, the self-employed had the lower rate of deviation from the trend in that sector. Linder (1983) analyzed the relationship between unemployment in individual industries and the occurrence of self-employment in those industries. Among all nonfarm industries, only the construction industry exhibited an increase in self-employment with a general decline in industry activity, but even in that case the relationship was not consistent. A statistically significant positive correlation between self-employment and unemployment in that industry was found for the period 1948–75. In the 1975–79 period, however, this relationship disappeared, at least statistically. At this point, the case for the business cycle as a major determinant of changes in self-employment is not strong.

DISPLACEMENT

If the case for the business cycle as a determinant of variations in the rate of self-employment appears weak, at least until additional research is performed, the case for industrial and technological displacement is even weaker. Studies of worker adjustment to permanent layoff in the United States and other countries have produced little evidence of a strong interest in self-employment as an adjustment strategy among displaced workers. Gordus, Jarley, and Ferman's review (1981) of the leading postwar studies of plant shutdowns and technological displacement report little evidence of self-employment as a response to job loss, with one exception. Mayer and Goldstein's (1964) study of eighty-one new businesses in Providence, Rhode Island, reported that the majority of owners were formerly manual workers in paid employment. Self-employment in one-fifth of the cases, however, was necessitated by layoff, not by a strong desire for independence and enhanced social status. A 1968 study (Palen and Fahey) that dealt explicitly with attitudes toward self-employment among displaced auto workers found these workers to have little general interest in starting their own businesses. [12] Such a strategy was regarded as "too chancy," possibly because 17 percent of the sample had had their own businesses at one time. Johnson (1981), in his review of studies of redundancy in British industries, also found little evidence that self-employment was an option for laid-off workers. According to his estimates, based on studies of business start-ups, only 2 percent of new businesses were initiated by unemployed individuals.

Several studies have proposed structural rigidities or anomalies in the face of business cycle changes as a source of increases in self-employment. Covick (1983), in an examination of increases in self-employment in Australia during recessions, proposed that barriers to full employment such as trade union wage policies or statutory minimum wages would promote an increase in self-employment. The implication of this thesis is that self-

---

12. An earlier study of auto workers also came to the conclusion that most workers held self-employment as an ideal rather than a practical option, which the author believes helped make life on the assembly line tolerable (Chinoy 1955).

employment becomes a form of underemployment. Blau (1987) used a general equilibrium analysis to test the wage rigidity hypothesis in an analysis of self-employment among men during the 1967–82 period. Increases in the real minimum wage during that period had a strong negative influence instead of the predicted positive influence on total self-employment. The coefficient for this variable for those persons with self-employment earnings only, the group that makes up the bulk of the self-employed, was also negative but not statistically significant.

INDUSTRIAL AND TECHNOLOGICAL CHANGE

In contrast to displacement, which is seen as a negative influence, changes in industrial structure and technology have been explored as positive influences on the growth of nonfarm self-employment. The simplest hypothesis follows from the fact that self-employment during the post–World War II period has been located predominantly in the service sector. The growth of this sector, so the argument goes, has carried self-employment along.

As a general proposition, there are at least two difficulties with this thesis. First, it provides no plausible explanation for the timing of the increase in self-employment. The upward trend in service sector employment was established long before the increase in nonfarm self-employment in the early 1970s. Second, in some important industries formerly characterized by self-employed entrepreneurs, the trend has been toward larger-scale business organizations. Although on average the growth of employment among the service industries has been half again as large as total private nonfarm employment, in some fields large-scale corporate organizations have replaced owner-managed enterprises. Banking, real estate, retail trade, and restaurants are familiar examples. As Stanback (1979) has noted, in a number of such industries, services have become standardized, which in turn has increased the degree to which they can be profitably delivered by large-scale organizations under centralized management and control. The capital requirements and the limits on a single individual's expertise and span of control make it difficult for self-employed entrepreneurs to compete with these organizations and thus decrease opportunities for self-employment in these industries.

Data on the industrial structure of nonfarm self-employment provide limited insight into the factors underlying the rates of change in self-employment (table 2.1). Wholesale and retail trade, real estate, and some professional services have grown more slowly than total nonfarm self-

TABLE 2.1 STRUCTURE OF SMALL BUSINESS: NONFARM SOLE PRO-
PRIETORS, SELECTED INDUSTRIES, 1977–1982 (in percent)

Industry	1977	1980	1982	% change
All nonfarm (in thousands)	8,042	9,347	9,812	22.0
Mining	0.9	1.3	1.4	94.3
Construction	12.4	11.5	12.3	21.0
General contractors	2.2	2.4	2.5	35.3
Specialty trades	9.1	8.3	9.3	23.4
Manufacturing	2.9	3.2	2.5	11.2
Transport, communication, public utilities	4.8	4.7	4.6	17.2
Trucking	3.4	3.4	3.3	18.5
Wholesale trade	3.8	3.5	2.8	−7.8
Retail trade	23.1	22.1	21.6	14.0
Food stores	2.0	1.8	2.0	26.6
Auto sales	2.9	2.2	1.6	−30.9
Apparel	0.9	0.7	0.7	−7.3
Eating and drinking	3.1	2.4	2.3	−10.6
Hobbies and toys	0.2	0.2	0.3	39.3
Gift shops	0.5	0.3	0.3	−25.5
Florists	0.4	0.3	0.3	−6.2
Direct selling	5.9	7.5	7.8	61.4
Finance	0.3	0.4	0.6	119.6
Securities brokers	0.2	0.4	0.4	121.8
Insurance	2.8	2.6	2.7	6.9
Real estate	8.0	8.3	6.2	−5.8
Services	41.1	41.1	43.6	29.5
Personal	8.4	7.9	7.9	13.7
Business	8.2	9.3	12.3	82.9
Auto repair	2.5	2.4	2.4	11.2
Amusement and recreation	3.5	3.3	3.0	2.6
Professional	11.7	11.1	12.2	26.2
Physicians	1.8	1.6	1.5	0.7
Dentists	1.0	0.9	0.8	−5.0
Nurses	0.6	0.5	0.5	−2.0
Legal services	2.0	1.9	2.3	35.1
Educational	1.6	1.9	1.6	27.6
Accounting	2.0	1.9	2.5	50.3

SOURCE: U.S.Treasury 1977, 1980, 1982.

employment or have lost ground in absolute terms. The relative importance of each area has also declined. In some but not all areas, standardization has been an important feature. Construction, finance, and some of the professional and business services, by contrast, have experienced above-average rates of growth of self-employment. Heterogeneity of demand for such services (i.e., individual, personalized attention to the particular demands of the clientele) may be a contributing factor in the latter instances.

The argument that the relative growth of the service sector is a major determinant of the growth of nonfarm self-employment is not altogether persuasive, certainly not with respect to timing. Recent within-sector developments, such as the growth of producers' services as a form of intermediate demand generated by changes in the organization and technology of the goods-producing industries, may be more significant. Goods production has become more heterogeneous and specialized. As a consequence, goods producers must choose between producing services internally in a quasi–custom-made process or purchasing them from firms that can supply them more cheaply because of their ability to specialize and/or enjoy economies of scale. Examples of services that may be contracted out to small businesses, including those run by the self-employed, are transport, communications, data processing, advertising, accounting, engineering, and architectural services (Tschetter 1987).

Technological change and innovation must always be considered when there are structural changes in labor markets. Technological advances may increase opportunities for self-employment, for example, by increasing opportunities for specialization, by increasing capital savings and thus reducing the cost of entry, and by changing the organization of production. Solid evidence of the influence of technology on self-employment and small business growth has been lacking, however.

Innovative information technology, principally the personal computer, has attracted a certain amount of attention. Birch and Gallagher (n.d.), for example, attribute much of the growth of small businesses, as measured by a significant rise in the rate and level of incorporations in the postwar period, to such innovations. Ginzberg, Noyelle, and Stanback (1986), by contrast, contend that personal computers have had no noticeable influence on the growth of small businesses. Blau (1987) found that an index of relative technology accounted for "fairly large shares of the observed increases in self-employment," along with changes in the industrial structure of employment. The data did not permit analysis of the changes in the aggregate index of technology, which Blau suggests should be a topic for future research. Thus far, his is the only study incorporating technology in its model of the growth of self-employment in the United States.

Institutional Developments

A variety of other factors, loosely categorized here as institutional rather than strictly market influences, may also have contributed to the increase in nonfarm self-employment in the 1970s. Some of these influences have received no attention in the relevant literature. In other cases, their effect has been ambiguous. Briefly examined here are changes in the organization and delivery of services and economic and social policies, including the effects of income taxes, minimum wage legislation, retirement policies and practices, and immigration policy. Government policies affecting the self-employed will be discussed further in chapter 5.

One potential influence on self-employment that has received no attention is franchising. Although the legal form adopted by franchised enterprises is not a matter of published record, it is likely that the great majority are sole proprietorships, especially where dealer rather than company ownership is indicated. There are two principal types of franchise: the product or trade name franchise, in which the business contracts to sell the product or services of a particular manufacturer, and the business format franchise.

Trade name franchises are characteristic of auto dealerships, soft drink wholesalers and distributors, and gasoline service stations. According to a report by the U.S. Department of Commerce (1987), this type of franchise has declined sharply in recent years, from 262,100 in 1972 to 158,460 in 1985. Various business and personal services, fast food chains, and real estate are among the leading industries characterized by the business format franchise. In contrast to trade name franchises, business format franchises have grown from 189,640 in 1972 to 322,174 in 1985. Franchises of this type tend toward a high degree of concentration.[13]

Franchised units may be owned exclusively by the franchisee or co-owned with the franchising company. In 1985, 81 percent of franchises were owned exclusively by the franchisee. For someone contemplating self-employment, franchising would seem to offer a number of advantages over owning one's business. In theory, franchisees enjoy comparative autonomy,

---

13. In 1983, fifty-five companies with one thousand or more units accounted for nearly half of sales through franchised establishments as well as a majority of such establishments (U.S. Department of Commerce 1987).

a tested business format, access to technical and management advice, a lower risk of failure, and perhaps easier access to finance. Under the business format arrangement, however, management autonomy is limited and a high degree of conformity and control may be exerted by the franchisor. Such control raises the question of whether the franchisee is truly self-employed or effectively a hired manager.

Despite its promise for the aspiring entrepreneur, franchising does not appear to have had a significant influence on the recent growth of self-employment in the United States. Although all types of franchises grew by 15 percent between 1969 and 1983 (U.S. Department of Commerce 1985), the absolute number at the end of the period, 441,181, was equivalent to only about 5 percent of total nonfarm self-employment. Independent, dealer-owned franchises over the same period actually declined, from a peak of 374,782 in 1973 to 355,392 in 1983, primarily because of a major decline in dealer-owned gasoline service stations. While rates of growth advanced rapidly in some particular lines of franchised business, mainly in services, non–service station dealer-owned franchises grew by only 52,000 units between 1972 and 1983 (table 2.2).

ORGANIZATIONAL CHANGE

Generally, self-employment rates have been higher among the so-called independent or classic professions than other occupational groups. If anything, however, the postwar trend among the professions has been away from self-employment toward more complex organizational forms. It should be noted that this development is not primarily the result of changes in legal status for tax and related advantages. Incorporation rates, in fact, have been relatively higher among nonprofessional managers of various kinds of businesses. Indeed, incorporation per se is likely to subject practitioners to regulation and auditing, possibly offsetting certain tax advantages. Increases in the capital cost of entry, including the cost of education and training as well as that of establishing a practice, and the marked increase in the number of women in the professions are more probable sources of the decline in self-employment in these fields.[14]

Unfortunately, it is possible to document changes in the setting or type of practice for only a few of the professions. Although the overall picture dur-

---

14. There is a popular but undocumented belief that the rising costs of malpractice insurance, as in the health professions, may also have contributed to the movement away from self-employment.

TABLE 2.2 DEALER-OWNED FRANCHISES, BY TYPE OF ESTABLISH-
MENT, 1972 AND 1983

Establishment	1972	1983	% change
All establishments	372,909	355,932	−4.6
Auto and truck sales	32,590	26,848	−17.6
Auto products	36,235	32,272	−10.9
Business services	11,925	39,987	235.3
Construction and home improvements	9,692	16,876	74.1
Convenience stores	4,007	6,237	55.6
Auto rentals	6,750	8,475	25.6
Equipment rentals	885	1,846	208.6
Nonfood retail stores	37,030	25,838	−30.2
Food retail stores	10,086	12,793	26.8
Soft drink bottlers	2,650	1,483	−44.5
Educational products	1,063	5,813	446.8
Restaurants	26,219	45,743	74.5
Gas stations	181,167	111,987	−38.2
Hotels, motels, camps	4,241	5,739	35.3
Laundries and dry cleaners	3,326	2,837	−14.7
Recreation and travel service	2,825	6,408	226.8
Miscellaneous	2,218	4,029	81.6

SOURCE: U.S. Department of Commerce 1987.

ing the 1970s and early 1980s is one of declining self-employment, there
are variations across the professions. Among dentists, for instance, the
number of solo practitioners (not necessarily equivalent to sole proprietors)
declined only moderately, from 77 percent of all practicing dentists in 1967
to 75 percent in 1981 and 72 percent in 1984 (American Dental Association
1969, 1983, 1987). Among lawyers, however, where the decline in self-
employment has been largely due to a general decline in private practice,
there was a drop in solo practices from 46 percent in 1960 to 33 percent in
1980. If private legal practice alone is considered, however, solo practice
shows a more modest rate of decline, from 52 percent in 1970 to 49 percent
in 1980 (American Bar Foundation 1985). Although women who enter private legal practice are more likely than men to be solo practitioners, they
have made a major contribution to the decline of self-employment in law
because they are more strongly inclined than men to eschew private practice. The quadrupling of the numbers of women in law since the 1950s has
enhanced this effect.

The pattern for physicians is much like that for lawyers. Between 1975 and 1983 the proportion of private practitioners in single-physician offices declined from 54.2 percent to 48.9 percent, while practices of five or more physicians increased from 16.8 to 22.7 percent (American Medical Association 1984). Parallel with the growth of practice size was a major increase in incorporated practices, which rose from 31 percent in 1975 to 54 percent in 1983 and to even higher levels in most specialized fields of medicine.

POLICIES AFFECTING SELF-EMPLOYMENT

The influence of retirement policy on self-employment has attracted more attention and research effort than any other single economic or institutional topic. Generally, the interest has been in predicting rates of retirement under the Social Security program. Levy (1975) found that in 1965 most nonfarm self-employed workers had previously worked in wage jobs, possibly in many cases under mandatory retirement policies. More recent studies have found only modest increases in self-employment rates among older wage workers—men, in most cases. All studies, however, report that the relatively higher self-employment rates among older workers result principally from a strong tendency among the self-employed to continue in the labor force after retirement, usually in the same occupation though in some cases on a part-time rather than a full-time basis (Quinn 1980; Fuchs 1982; Daum 1984; Parnes and Less 1985; Iams 1987). The most recent study, based on the New Beneficiary Survey by the Social Security Administration, reports a self-employment rate of 37 percent for men and 12 percent for women among Social Security beneficiaries. In both cases this rate is considerably higher than that of the nonretiree population (Iams 1987).

Wage and salary workers are more likely than the self-employed to withdraw completely from the labor force after retirement. Among wage and salary workers who continued to work after retirement about 23 percent did so as self-employed workers and, in contrast to those who were previously self-employed, they worked in occupations and industries that were different from their preretirement pattern. Blau's finding (1987) that increases in Social Security benefits affected entry into self-employment only for those not completely dependent on self-employment earnings is consistent with such observations.

Several studies (Blau 1987; Evans and Leighton 1987; Long 1982) have examined the influence of changes in marginal income tax rates on the growth of self-employment.[15] Because, as noted earlier, self-employment and small business offer relatively good opportunity for underreporting taxable income, an upward movement in marginal rates might be expected to increase the interest in self-employment. None of the studies referred to have examined actual changes in tax rates, however, nor have they been based on individual observation of rates of tax liability. Blau, for example, entered two different assumed marginal rates into his model with apparently contradictory results.[16] Evans and Leighton included income tax and Social Security payroll taxes in their analysis of self-employment growth; again, the results are not easy to interpret. Increases in the index of federal income taxes had the predictable effect of increasing self-employment, but this effect was stronger on incorporated than unincorporated self-employed men. By contrast, increases in Social Security tax rates decreased the rate of self-employment among the unincorporated while increasing the rate among the incorporated. For women, the Social Security tax effect was a mirror image of its effect on men. Long's study of self-employed men, based on the 1970 census, found a statistically significant positive tax effect after controlling for variables such as marital status and country of birth.

Blau (1987) tested the proposition that self-employment would provide a route around wage rigidity, hypothesizing that workers rationed out of wage jobs because of the minimum wage and, presumably, having lower reservation wages would become self-employed. The empirical test, however, found an unexplained negative effect on self-employment. One may speculate that workers who benefit from a minimum wage are probably not good candidates for self-employment and, further, that for such workers a minimum wage job may be preferable to the uncertainties of self-employment. In this context, it might be useful to explore the effect across industries of differences in unionization rates on propensities to become self-employed.

The change in immigration policy effected by the Immigration Act of 1965 may also have helped produce a rise in the rate of self-employment, for two reasons. First, the rate of legal immigration increased from its pre-1965 level of about 300,000 persons annually to levels between 25 and 50 percent higher (McKay 1989). Net immigration doubled its pre-1965 aver-

---

15. Other studies have made hypothetical references to the tax effect but have not attempted empirical tests.

16. A high rate had a positive effect on self-employment, but a lower rate had a negative effect and, when removed in the analysis, tended to dampen the overall effect of marginal tax rates.

age annual rate during the 1970s, increasing to 25 percent of total population growth (U.S. Congress Select Commission 1980). Second, the new law admitted immigrants on the basis of family relationship and scarcity of domestic sources of skilled labor.

More important, perhaps, than these two factors was the significant shift in the immigrants' countries of origin. From 1950 to 1960, the bulk of immigrants came from European countries or countries with European histories, such as Italy, the United Kingdom, Canada, and Germany. In the post-1965 period, immigration was predominantly from Asia, with Taiwan, Korea, and the Philippines accounting for the largest single shares of total immigration (U.S. Congress 1980). In 1965, Asians accounted for 7 percent of total immigration to the United States; by 1981, that proportion had reached 44 percent and showed no sign of decline (Light and Bonacich 1988). Groups from Asia appear to have a relatively high propensity for self-employment, possibly because of initial language handicaps and other sociocultural disadvantages. Data and studies bearing on this issue are scarce. What literature there is will be examined in chapter 4 in the discussion of subgroups in the self-employed work force.

Summary and Conclusions

A variety of factors bearing on the increase in nonfarm self-employment in the 1970s were reviewed in this chapter, including micro-oriented demographic and social influences on the one hand and broad structural and institutional changes on the other. No single influence stands out as being the primary factor in the recent growth of self-employment, nor is it clear exactly how some of the factors have affected shifts from employment to self-employment.

The demographic and social characteristics of self-employment, with one exception, appear to have been much the same in the 1970s and later as they were in earlier periods. Entry into self-employment is still basically a mid–work life phenomenon, following substantial experience in the labor force as an employee. The self-employed also seem to resemble wage workers in other measurable respects. It may be, however, that changes have occurred in factors that are less accessible to measurement, such as shifts in attitudes toward autonomy, flexibility in working hours, willingness to accept economic risk, and even work itself. The marked increase in the participation of women in self-employment, ignored in most studies, suggests the probability of an increase in the importance of nonpecuniary factors. Future research will be needed to test this relationship, however.

Various studies of structural influences such as changes in the rate of economic growth and in the organization of production, the growth of the service industries, and advances in technology were reviewed. Again, the results were implausible or ambiguous. Service sector and other industry growth preceded the upturn in self-employment, and in general these areas did not expand more rapidly during the period of faster growth in self-employment. Technological changes, especially in computer and information technology, probably facilitated the entry of some groups into self-employment via the so-called electronic cottage, but the overall influence of these changes remains unclear. Covick (1983) and others have raised the perennial question of whether a marked increase in self-employment is a response to a declining rate of aggregate demand and employment (i.e., disequilibrium) rather than a secular change driven by such factors as changes in production and consumption patterns. As Covick suggests, earnings relationships (discussed in chapter 3) may be the key to an acceptable answer.

Various studies of institutional changes bearing on self-employment were also reviewed. Franchising in a variety of service industries, the organization and delivery of health services, and increases in statutory minimum wages all appear to be moving workers away from self-employment. Changes in tax and retirement policies, however, had no clear-cut effect on changes in the rate of self-employment.

Research on the recent growth of nonfarm self-employment has just begun. Only a handful of studies have approached the issue head-on, so to speak; in most studies, self-employment is a secondary issue. At this point it is impossible to declare with any high degree of certainty that the growth of self-employment represents a significant and lasting change in the nature and behavior of labor markets. Furthermore, there is the apparent and counterintuitive paradox of the growth of self-employment in the face of declining earnings, suggestive of a supply- rather than a demand-driven phenomenon. The next chapter will focus on earnings differences, the occurrence and explanation of which will take account of the employment changes discussed in this chapter.

Chapter Three

Earnings and Self-Employment

In an ideal market, differences in the price of services for labor of equal productivity should not exist. Whether one works as an employee or is self-employed should make no difference: the return to one's labor should be equal.[1] Observed differences in earnings between otherwise comparable labor stimulate our interest because they confound theoretical expectations and because they are important in understanding from a historical viewpoint how labor markets adjust to changes in social and economic environments.

The preceding chapters documented the upturn in nonfarm self-employment and discussed a variety of possible determinants of that growth. This chapter is essentially a continuation of that discussion. Understanding earnings relationships between the self-employed and their wage and salary counterparts can be valuable in deciding whether the recent gains in self-employment are mainly demand- or supply-driven or whether they are the product of changes in labor market structures and institutions.

The central fact about the earnings of the self-employed in the recent period of expansion is their decline from a relatively more favorable level to a relatively less favorable level in comparison with the average earnings of employees. A fair comparison requires a measure of earnings common to the groups being compared. The studies reviewed in this chapter are not consistent in this regard so it is necessary to qualify generalizations about earnings relationships by calling attention to the measurement differences. A brief discussion of the measurement issue is followed by a discussion of

---

1. The meaning of equality is, of course, a matter of theory or definition since the reported monetary payment for labor may constitute less than full compensation. The nonmonetary component is usually unobservable, but it is estimated to vary greatly among individuals and occupational groups.

the current earnings position of self-employed workers, historical changes in that position, and variations in the relative earnings attributable to such factors as age, gender, education, occupation, and industry. The chapter concludes with a review of the handful of analytical studies of self-employment earnings and some tentative conclusions.

Measurement of Earnings from Self-Employment

Problems in using observed or reported earnings from published sources as analytical tools are common for all labor force groups, including the self-employed. The most common problem, perhaps, is that aggregation may conceal important information such as the gender, schooling, or occupational composition underlying earnings differences. Another common problem is the adequacy of the sampling procedure, since most sources of earnings data are based on samples even where enumeration would have been possible, as with data from the population censuses or the social insurance system.

In addition, earnings in self-employment have their own particular measurement problems. Self-employment takes place either as an unincorporated or an incorporated enterprise. As noted earlier, the incorporated self-employed are treated in published sources as employees, though they can be identified from the tapes of the Census and the Current Population Survey. The earnings of this group are distinctly greater, on average, than the earnings of the unincorporated self-employed. Most studies ignore this difference, however, because the overall effect on earnings comparisons would probably be quite small.[2]

Many individuals derive their incomes from several sources, including returns to physical capital. Wage earners in the construction trades, for example, usually own their tools. An estimation of the discounted value of this income would be quite difficult, but, again, the effect in most cases is probably small and is therefore ignored. Nevertheless, it would be helpful to know whether the income derived by the self-employed from returns to physical capital is substantially greater, as is frequently assumed, or comparable in relative terms to the nonlabor sources of income of the average wage earner.

The most serious problem in comparing the earnings of the self-employed and wage earners is the relative reliability of reported earnings.

---

2. The incorporated self-employed are more likely to include entrepreneurs in the classical sense. The majority are managers of small businesses.

As noted in the appendix, the self-employed tend to underreport income and earnings as a method of reducing their tax liability. While there are estimates of the overall degree of underreporting, I know of no information on how underreporting varies according to the differing characteristics of the self-employed.

Studies do not address these measurement problems in a consistent manner. Fredland and Little (1981) omitted the incorporated self-employed but used family income, including income from nonbusiness and nonlabor sources, as the measure of comparability between wage earners and the self-employed. Because Blau (1987) felt appropriate adjustments could not be made to the earnings of the two groups, he aggregated the incomes of the incorporated and unincorporated. Form (1985) and Evans and Leighton (1987) reported the earnings of the two groups separately. The latter study, however, was more concerned with the problem of distinguishing self-employed workers whose earnings were solely dependent on self-employment income from individuals whose earnings to varying degrees combined self-employment and employee incomes. Form included profits as well as wages in the earnings of the self-employed. Becker (1984) excluded implicit income from his measure of self-employment earnings on the assumption that such income was not available to wage earners.[3]

Although underreporting of earnings is widely acknowledged to be a serious problem, only one study has attempted to come to terms with it directly. Form (1985) adjusted profits reported by the self-employed to the 1970 census by an across-the-board increase of 30 percent. This arbitrary procedure may account in part for the finding of a 9 percent advantage in favor of proprietors' income as compared with that of employees.[4]

Earnings from Self-Employment

All but a few post–World War II studies of self-employment report that the earnings of the self-employed are, on average, less than those of individuals who are employed by others. Although Form (1985) reported about a 9 percent advantage for the self-employed in 1970, his income measure, as noted above, included profits as well as labor income. Borjas (1986) reported higher earnings from self-employment in 1980 for men in each of

---

3. Such as the use of a business car for personal travel, or the income attributable to using one's home as a place of business.

4. As noted below, except for the magnitude of the earnings differential, the self-employed, on average, enjoyed an earnings advantage over wage and salary workers prior to the 1970s.

twelve ethnic or racial groups.[5] These reports contrast sharply, however, with the findings reported in other sources for the postwar period. For example, the Bureau of Labor Statistics to date has issued four reports on the self-employed, each of which records and comments on the lower earnings of the self-employed (Bregger 1963; Ray 1975; Fain 1980; Becker 1984). The data source for each of these reports was the Current Population Survey, on which estimates of the labor force and employment are based. According to Becker's study, the average earnings of the self-employed in 1982 were equal to about 70 percent of the earnings of wage and salary workers, despite the longer workweek of the former.

Special tabulations prepared for the Small Business Administration emphasize how earnings comparisons hinge on whether individuals are solely dependent on a single or multiple sources of earnings and on the type of self-employment. CPS data for May 1983, reporting on annual earnings in 1982, showed that full-time, full-year unincorporated self-employed workers wholly dependent on their businesses for income received median annual earnings of $13,134, while full-time wage and salary workers without side businesses reported median earnings of $17,992, approximately 37 percent more (SBA, *State of Small Business, 1986*). The unincorporated self-employed who combined their businesses with wage and salary jobs earned half again as much as those solely dependent on self-employment, while the annual earnings of the incorporated self-employed were almost two and one-half times greater.

Data from other sources for approximately the same year tend to confirm the generally less favorable earnings position of the self-employed. Survey of Income and Program Participation data for 1983, for example, show that the annualized earnings of men working full time in unincorporated businesses were 67 percent those of men dependent solely on paid employment (Haber, Lamas, and Lichtenstein 1987).[6] For women, according to the same source, the ratio of earnings in unincorporated self-employment to paid employment was 0.31. Internal Revenue Service data based on income tax returns show that in 1982 the average before-tax net income of nonfarm sole proprietors was about $10,150 for those enterprises with net income. Even the gross receipts of those enterprises were, on average, only a little more than $50,000 (U.S. Treasury 1982). These data, however, cannot be

---

5. His six groups, whites, blacks, Asians, Mexicans, Cubans, and other Hispanics, were further subdivided into native-born or immigrant.

6. The earnings were reported for two quarterly periods covering the last six months of 1983, then annualized for 1983.

corrected for differences in the length of the work year, among other factors, nor do they separate labor income from returns to capital and property.

Nonagricultural self-employed workers in most other countries also tend to receive less for their labor than employees. An OECD report (1986) shows that the ratio of median earnings of self-employed workers to wage and salary workers in most of the eleven countries studied was less than 1.0; in Finland, Sweden, and Japan the ratio was well below the ratio in the United States. Only in the Federal Republic of Germany did self-employed workers receive higher earnings than wage and salary workers in that year.

The Decline in Relative Earnings

The earnings gap in the United States between wage and salary workers and the self-employed to the disadvantage of the latter is a relatively recent development. Earnings data for the earlier post–World War II years are more favorable to the self-employed; indeed, most of the studies of the 1950s and 1960s show an earnings advantage for the self-employed. Phillips (1962) reported higher annual earnings for the nonfarm self-employed than for wage workers, regardless of gender. Leveson (1968) constructed a series comparing in 1957–59 dollars the real before-tax annual incomes of the unincorporated self-employed and wage and salary workers. In every year of the period 1947–62, the adjusted real incomes of the self-employed exceeded the incomes of wage and salary workers. In addition, the ratios for professional workers were above those of nonprofessional workers.

The erosion of the earnings advantage of self-employed workers may have begun sometime in the early 1960s. For the combined sample in Leveson's study, the annual real earnings of the unincorporated self-employed in 1962 were only 8 percent greater than the earnings of wage and salary workers, whereas in the 1947–49 period they were 30 percent higher. Several years later, using Social Security data for 1965, Levy (1975) found that the earnings gap had virtually disappeared. The median annual earnings for nonfarm self-employed men were only fifty-two dollars higher than those of wage and salary workers. For nonfarm self-employed women, the reported advantage over wage and salary workers in that year was only eight dollars.

The disappearance of the earnings advantage of the self-employed cannot be precisely dated, however. Social Security earnings data, which are among the more reliable earnings measures, indicate that until the mid-1970s the earnings of the self-employed not only exceeded but held a nearly

TABLE 3.1. ESTIMATED QUINQUENNIAL ANNUAL AVERAGE EARN-INGS, BY CLASS OF WORKER, 1951–1988[a]

Period	Wage and salary	Self-employed	Self/wage
1951–54	$2,621	$3,890	1.48
1955–59	3,155	3,926	1.24
1960–64	3,743	4,664	1.25
1965–69	4,643	5,355	1.15
1970–74	6,220	8,505	1.35
1975–79	8,925	10,977	1.23
1980–84	13,345	11,879	.90
1985–88	16,958	13,374	.79

SOURCE: Computed from U.S. Department of Health and Human Services 1989.
[a]Coverage of self-employment under the law began in 1951.

constant advantage over the earnings of wage and salary workers (table 3.1). Only in the 1980–84 period did the average annual earnings of the self-employed begin to fall below the earnings of wage and salary workers.

Time series of comparable earnings relationships in other countries are generally not accessible through published sources. Covick (1983) constructed an earnings series that shows that the earnings of the self-employed relative to average incomes from all income sources experienced a steep decline in Australia in the period 1966–79. In certain industries at the end of the period, however, notably finance, personal services, and recreation, the incomes of the self-employed still exceeded those of wage and salary workers. Although probably only a coincidence, the overall rate of decline in that country steepened markedly after 1973–74, as it did in the United States. The ratio of average self-employment incomes to average employment incomes fell from 1.53 in 1966–67 to 0.94 in 1978–79. Again, as in the United States, this development was concurrent with relatively large gains in nonfarm self-employment.

The data presented thus far provoke two related questions: why are earnings in self-employment lower on average than the earnings of wage and salary workers; and why did the earnings of the self-employed in the United States fall in absolute and, therefore, relative terms during the period just after the end of World War II, when the self-employed enjoyed a substantial earnings advantage over wage and salary workers? Furthermore, if we consider the growth of nonwage compensation in the wage and salary sector, the income gap may be even larger than wage measures alone indicate.

Earnings Variations and Contributing Factors

There is, as always, the question of the reliability of the earnings measures, especially given the propensity of the self-employed to underreport their earnings. The degree to which earnings are underreported and how such underreporting varies according to the characteristics of the self-employed, however, is unknown. The following sections explore the overall earnings difference along a number of known dimensions, including demographic and social variables, work-leisure patterns, and occupational and industrial earnings differentials.

DIFFERENCES IN TIME WORKED

Differences in time worked, of course, must be accounted for in earnings comparisons. The greater the time span of the unit of measure, the more important the need to insure comparability in the quantity of work performed. Since it is well known that self-employed workers tend to work longer weekly hours and more weeks in the year than wage and salary workers, it is necessary to correct for this difference between the two types of employment so as to provide an accurate reading of the difference in the supply price of labor. Data that link earnings and work time are not generally available on a year-to-year basis; however, some information can be found in Census and similar sources. In 1969, according to the 1970 Census of Population, average annual earnings of nonfarm self-employed workers were almost 70 percent greater than the annual earnings of nonfarm wage and salary workers. Only 53 percent of the latter, however, worked full-time, full-year jobs, while 83 percent of the self-employed were so engaged. Using a crude procedure whereby one applies to the earnings difference the ratio of the proportions of self-employed and wage and salary workers working a full year, the advantage of the self-employed falls to only 7 percent.[7] Published 1980 Census data unfortunately do not permit a repetition of this adjustment procedure.

Several reports (Fain 1980; Becker 1984) indicate that the average number of hours worked per week by the self-employed now closely approxi-

---

7. Most studies reporting earnings comparisons between the self-employed and wage earners simply refer to the longer workweeks and work years of the self-employed, but without attempting adjustment for this difference. Evans and Leighton (1987) suggest that efforts to estimate hourly wage rates may be misleading because self-employed workers have no incentive to maintain accurate records of time worked and, further, because their mix of work and leisure can differ radically from that of the average wage or salary worker.

TABLE 3.2. MEDIAN ANNUAL EARNINGS OF WAGE AND SALARY WORKERS AND THE SELF-EMPLOYED, BY QUARTERS OF COVERAGE, SELECTED YEARS, 1955–1976

Year	All wage and salary	Four-quarter wage and salary	All self-employed	Self-employed/ all wage and salary	Self-employed/ four-quarter wage and salary
1955	$2,383	$3,464	$2,397	1.01	.69
1958	2,629	3,692	2,777	1.06	.75
1961	2,876	4,052	3,017	1.05	.74
1964	3,224	4,511	3,499	1.08	.78
1967	3,660	5,080	4,472	1.22	.88
1970	4,317	6,194	5,104	1.18	.82
1973	5,063	7,274	6,537	1.29	.90
1976	6,156	8,919	7,135	1.16	.76

SOURCES: 1955–76, U.S. Department of Health and Human Services, *Social Security Bulletin, Annual Statistical Supplement,* 1977–79.

mate those worked by wage and salary workers. It is possible, thus, that the decline in the relative earnings of the self-employed may be attributable in some part to a change in their work-leisure preferences in favor of an increase in leisure or nonwork time. While this hypothesis cannot be directly tested in the absence of comparative data on time worked, Social Security data (table 3.2) for a limited period suggests that it may be invalid. Full-year wage workers, whose earnings are taxed and reported quarterly for the period 1955–76, are compared with self-employed workers, whose earnings are reported only once a year. Although the part-time self-employed cannot be distinguished from their full-time counterparts in this data source, there appears to have been a general upward trend in the earnings of the self-employed relative to those of wage and salary workers during the period. The higher and increasing ratio of the earnings of the self-employed compared to those of all wage and salary workers could be interpreted to mean that, other things being equal, it is the latter group rather than the former that has been increasing its leisure time.[8]

---

8. In an interesting study of the effect of on-the-job leisure on productivity and wages, Hamermesh (1990) shows that compared with employees solely dependent on wages, the self-employed in a sample that kept time-use diaries in 1975–76 earned twice as much, worked almost 10 percent longer workweeks, but took only half as much break time during working hours. Although the sample is quite small with an "n" of 343, including only 32 self-employed, the comparison suggests that if this group of self-employed are representative, maximization of money income is still a very strong work incentive.

Given the number of women who have entered self-employment in the United States and other industrialized countries, it is especially important to assess the role of gender in hours worked and, inferentially, in earnings differences between the two types of employment. As noted above, there has been a convergence in the number of hours worked per week between the self-employed and employees in the United States. Gender differences may be contributing to this convergence as larger numbers of women have entered self-employment and, in particular, part-time and casual self-employment.

A recent survey reported that the difference in work time among male full-time business owners was nearly 29 percent higher than among women business owners. By contrast, the gender difference among paid full-time employees was only 17 percent (Haber, Lamas, and Lichtenstein 1987).

Data on comparative earnings by both class of worker and gender are not available for most other industrialized countries. In general, it appears that in most other countries there has been no tendency toward convergence in time worked between employees and the self-employed. Moreover, as an OECD survey of eighteen countries covering the period 1973–84 shows, even when work-time patterns are broken down by gender as well as class of work, the self-employed work longer hours than wage and salary workers (OECD 1986).

DEMOGRAPHIC AND SOCIAL FACTORS

Comparative data on other dimensions of earnings of the self-employed are scanty, but it is possible to make a few generalizations using variables such as age, gender, education, racial or ethnic identity, industry, occupation, and legal form of self-employment. For most personal and social characteristics, there are virtually no outstanding differences in earnings patterns between the self-employed and wage and salary workers. Occupational and industrial employment and legal form of business, however, tend more sharply to differentiate the self-employed from wage and salary workers.

AGE AND EARNINGS PATTERNS

The age and earnings profiles of wage and salary workers and the self-employed show a positive relationship with age for both types of employment. A special tabulation of 1980 census data shows average incomes increasing with age for both types of employment up to about age sixty,

TABLE 3.3. MEDIAN ANNUAL EARNINGS OF FULL-TIME, FULL-YEAR NONFARM WORKERS, BY SEX, RACE, AND CLASS OF WORKER, 1983

Race	Male			Female		
	Wage and salary	Self-employed	Ratio	Wage and salary	Self-employed	Ratio
All races	$22,463	$18,901	.84	$13,344	$8,673	.65
White	23,128	19,157	.83	13,557	8,389	.62
Black	15,875	18,275	1.15	11,985	N.A.	—
Hispanic	16,022	14,086	.88	11,328	N.A.	—

SOURCE: U.S. Bureau of the Census 1984a.

after which there is a sharp decline. The 1979 incomes recorded in the census are larger at every age for white wage and salary earners, though the reverse was true for nonwhites over sixty (SBA, *State of Small Business, 1985*).

EARNINGS DIFFERENCES BY GENDER AND RACE

Earnings differences by gender and racial group also transcend types of employment. In 1983, self-employed women earned not only less than men regardless of class of work but also less than women employed in wage and salary jobs (table 3.3). All black and Hispanic workers, both self-employed and wage and salary, earned less than white workers. These estimates are based on individuals working in full-time, full-year employment.

Earnings differences between men and women in the two types of employment have taken slightly divergent paths in recent years. Data assembled by the Small Business Administration (*State of Small Business, 1986*) show that during the 1974–84 period the ratio of women's to men's earnings in self-employment was virtually constant at about 0.50. During the same period, women employed in wage and salary jobs made larger gains in earnings, increasing the ratio of their earnings relative to men from about 0.46 to 0.53. Earnings patterns of self-employed women and minorities will be discussed further in chapter 4.

HUMAN CAPITAL INVESTMENTS

Both wage and salary workers and the self-employed gain from educational investments, but the former appear to have higher rates of return from given levels of educational attainment (Bauman 1987). According to an SBA re-

port, however, full-time self-employed workers are somewhat better educated than wage and salary workers (SBA, *State of Small Business, 1986*).
In May 1983, 28 percent of the unincorporated self-employed had four or
more years of college, compared with 24 percent of wage and salary workers without other sources of labor income. Despite the educational advantage and the presumed advantage of greater experience, indicated by the
age difference of the self-employed, the 1980 Census records that in absolute terms the average income of wage and salary workers exceeded the
income of the self-employed at every level of education (SBA, *State of
Small Business, 1985*).

Various studies of the relationship between human capital investments
such as formal education and vocational training and earnings have tested
for the possibility that employers use educational credentials as a relatively
inexpensive screen in the hiring and promotion of workers. Since the self-
employed sell their labor directly, their earnings patterns should provide a
control for testing for the presence of screening, as suggested by Wolpin
(1977). It may also be hypothesized that, because the self-employed are not
subject to such screening, the return to their labor from given levels of
education and other human capital investments ought to be greater than for
those working for others.[9]

No consensus emerges from the few studies that have investigated the
relative human capital returns of self-employed and wage and salary workers. Form (1985) found that education did not have a statistically significant
effect on the earnings of either group. Vocational training benefited the
self-employed more than wage workers, although vocational preparation
generally had a negative impact on the earnings of both groups. In their
study of prime working-age males, omitting professional workers, Fredland
and Little (1981) found no statistically significant difference between the
two types of employment in their gains from general education. A significant difference was observed in that study, however, in the gains from vocational education, which favored wage and salary workers. Evans and
Leighton (1987) calculated annual percentage rates of return for the male
cohort of their study during the period 1966–81. Compared with wage
workers, the self-employed experienced higher returns from educational attainment and management and skill training but lower returns from previous
wage experience and professional training. The authors comment that the

---

9. In formal theoretical terms, the self-employed would not be subject to monopsonistic
exploitation because of market imperfections.

TABLE 3.4. RATIO OF MEDIAN ANNUAL EARNINGS OF FULL-TIME, FULL-YEAR NONFARM SELF-EMPLOYED TO WAGE AND SALARY WORKERS, BY GENDER AND OCCUPATION, 1982

Occupations	Male	Female
Managerial and professional	.86	.58
Technical and sales	.73	.57
Services	.75	.53
Crafts	.65	.54
Operatives and laborers	.70	.54

SOURCE: Becker 1984.

returns from wage experience, after controlling for self-selection into self-employment, were even lower, suggesting that workers with relatively low productivity characteristics tend to move into self-employment.

EARNINGS BY INDUSTRY AND OCCUPATION

Occupational differences in earnings by class of worker are even less accessible in published sources than other labor market dimensions. Nevertheless, in the most recent published information, the self-employed appear to fare less well than employees. Becker (1984), drawing on CPS data for 1982, reported that earnings of self-employed men ranged from 65 percent of the earnings of wage and salary workers in the skilled manual occupations to 86 percent of the earnings of men in managerial and professional jobs (table 3.4). Among women, however, the contrast in earnings was almost invariant with respect to occupational group.

Earnings by industry and class of worker, as in the case of occupational data, are accessible only through special tabulations of Census or CPS files. In table 3.5, the net incomes of sole proprietors who reported net income to the IRS have been used as a proxy for the earnings of the self-employed. By comparison with male workers, self-employed and employees, the earnings of sole proprietors are lower in every industry. Only in two industries, mining and professional and related services, do the incomes of sole proprietors exceed those of women workers in those industries.

Earnings also differ by legal form of business organization and by whether the self-employed employ others. In both cases, though not necessarily coinciding, earnings of the incorporated self-employed tend to exceed the earnings of both wage and salary workers and the unincorporated self-employed. For example, in 1982 the median earnings of incorporated self-

TABLE 3.5. MONEY EARNINGS, BY INDUSTRY AND GENDER, OF FULL-TIME, PRIVATE NONFARM WORKERS AND AVERAGE NET INCOMES OF SOLE PROPRIETORS, 1982

	All workers		Sole proprietors	
Industry average	Male	Female	No. of returns[b]	Net incomes
All industries	$23,637[a]	$14,327[a]	6,761,405	$10,153
Agriculture, forestry, etc.	11,131	6,573	170,380	7,662
Mining	32,010	19,819	58,610	27,315
Construction	21,663	14,939	965,852	8,289
Manufacturing	24,786	14,244	140,256	10,342
Transport, communication, etc.	25,142	18,089	310,398	8,502
Wholesale trade	25,532	14,914	186,768	13,154
Retail trade	17,747	11,009	1,072,703	8,338
Finance, insurance, real estate	28,667	14,469	622,433	12,389
Business and repair service	21,956	15,499	1,187,289	8,440
Personal services	15,694	9,159	608,209	4,797
Professional and related services	27,781	15,257	983,744	18,406

SOURCES: All workers, U.S. Bureau of the Census 1984a; sole proprietors' net income calculated by the author from U.S. Treasury 1984.

[a]Includes farming.
[b]Businesses with net income only.

employed workers were $30,048, in contrast to $17,992 for wage and salary workers and $13,134 for the unincorporated self-employed (SBA, *State of Small Business, 1986*). Such differences are probably due to occupational and industrial differences in employment and, perhaps, corresponding differences in human and physical capital. Researching the influence of payroll employment on the self-employed owner's earnings, Ben-Porath (1986) found that self-employed men in Israel who employed others enjoyed an earnings advantage over the nonemploying self-employed. Calculations from IRS data (U.S. Treasury 1981) on sole proprietorships show that between 1965 and 1980, payroll expenses as a proportion of gross business receipts declined from about 11 percent to near 8 percent, which would be consistent with the decline in the earnings of the self-employed.

Earnings Analysis

As observed at the opening of this chapter, in theory, earnings differentials should be unaffected by whether one works for others or for oneself. Indeed, such prominent observers of the labor market as Douglas (1957) and

Hicks (1966) assumed that the average market-determined wage of employees is also the expected wage of the self-employed. As yet, however, empirical investigation of this assumption is not the focus of most of the studies examined. Analysis of the difference in earnings between wage earners and the self-employed is either subordinated to another issue, such as the social class of the self-employed (Wright 1979; Form 1985), or a component of a related matter, such as theories of entrepreneurship (Johnson 1977; Evans and Leighton 1989). Brief reference has been made to these and other studies earlier in this chapter. In this section, I attempt to place the findings of the more useful studies in a theoretical context.

Assuming the self-employed and the wage earner have similar or equal potential for productivity, in what respects relevant to earnings may they differ? The obvious major difference, in principle, is in their ownership, responsibility, and control over physical capital. Two hypotheses that follow from this observation propose relatively higher earnings for the self-employed. First, control and ownership of physical capital imply that the entire yield of the capital investment will belong to its owner and that there will be a strong incentive to utilize plant, equipment, and tools more efficiently. Second, the self-employed worker, as entrepreneur, should be compensated for the risk of loss of capital and, as worker, for job loss should the business venture fail.

The few studies that consider the relationship of capital ownership to earnings are not favorable to the self-employed. Leveson (1968) found that ownership and control of nonlabor inputs raised the relative annual earnings of self-employed men above those of wage earners by about 10 percent, but that a subgroup of self-employed retail managers earned less than their salaried counterparts. Daum (1984) found higher levels of job satisfaction among a cohort of middle-aged self-employed males, and Fredland and Little (1985) reported a stronger feeling of job control and autonomy in the same group. Neither study, however, related these findings directly to earnings differences after controlling for other variables. Fredland and Little observed with some surprise that despite significantly greater business assets, the mean incomes of the self-employed were not significantly different from those of wage earners. The same study also suggests that the self-employed are not great risk-takers but move cautiously into full-time self-employment.

The theory of compensating differentials[10] suggests that greater control over both physical capital and one's labor may provide a source of real income that offsets or compensates for relatively lower monetary returns.

---

10. See any contemporary textbook on labor economics, e.g., Ehrenberg and Smith 1991.

None of the studies discussed here examine this possibility, though Fredland and Little (1985) and Evans and Leighton (1989) employ a measure of job control in explaining entry into self-employment.

One of the problems in testing the foregoing propositions is the lack of information about the context of the earnings relationship. Two examples will illustrate this point. First, perhaps as many as 40 percent of small businesses are financed from family and personal resources (SBA, *State of Small Business, 1986*). In combination with the relatively low levels of business receipts, this suggests that the scale of enterprise and the quality of capital at the disposal of the self-employed business yield relatively low absolute returns regardless of how efficiently they are employed. The second example is the effect of the level of business activity on the earnings of the self-employed. In a recession, when there are fewer job vacancies, a self-employed worker may accept lower earnings as a means of preserving his or her capital investment and as an alternative to unemployment when he or she is not eligible for insurance benefits. In such circumstances the self-employed worker is effectively underemployed.

EARNINGS MODELS

Five studies to which I have frequently referred have attempted to compare the determinants of earnings from self-employment with the earnings of wage and salary workers. With one exception (Fredland and Little 1981), all the studies include the same independent variables to calculate the earnings regressions of the wage earners and the self-employed. Four studies are based on samples of men drawn from the census (Brock, Evans, and Phillips 1986), the Current Population Survey (Blau 1987), or the National Longitudinal Survey (Fredland and Little 1981; Evans and Leighton 1989). Form (1985) used 1970 census data, which included both men and women in the analysis. A sixth study (Quinn 1980) focused on the labor force participation patterns of older self-employed workers but also modeled the determinants of that group's earnings. A few other studies have made reference to comparative earnings but have not analyzed the differences. In this section, I describe the models and results of these studies (excluding Quinn).

Although only Fredland and Little (1981) focus primarily on earnings relationships, all five principal studies aim to some degree to understand the recent changes in the earnings rates of the self-employed. Two of the studies (Fredland and Little 1981; Evans and Leighton 1989) may be characterized as human capital earnings models, even though additional variables such as type or region of location are included as controls. Fredland and Little's study focuses on the role of education and training as a screen rather than as a human capital investment that enhances earning capacity. The self-employed are assumed to have no incentive to invest in academic or vocational credentials as a screen since they sell the output of their labor directly.[11] The effects of five education and training variables on the earnings of nonfarm self-employed workers and their wage and salary counterparts were analyzed. The expectation that the returns from general training would be higher for the self-employed, because they are required to perform a greater variety of tasks, was confirmed. Formal schooling yielded higher returns to the self-employed, as hypothesized, but the removal of professional workers from that sample reduced the earnings advantage over wage and salary workers to almost nothing.[12] Self-employed workers gained more than wage and salary workers from on-the-job training and experience for relatively short periods. On all other human capital variables, wage and salary workers and the self-employed were very much alike. Overall, the authors conclude, there was no strong support for the screening hypothesis, especially in view of the higher mean levels of education among the self-employed.

Evans and Leighton (1989), in the other human capital model, included previous military, business, and wage experience (i.e., various forms of on-the-job training) and education. The self-employed experienced a higher yield than wage workers from formal education, even after eliminating professional workers. The returns from wage work that carried over into self-employment were lower than the returns from previous wage experience in wage work and lower than the returns from self-employment in wage work. One interpretation of this result, the authors propose, is that workers with relatively poorer human capital endowments tend to become self-employed. It would be useful to know just how relevant previous experience in wage employment is to self-employment. Again, the human capital approach did not further our understanding of the earnings of the self-employed.

Two other efforts to understand the earnings of the self-employed are essentially eclectic and only by implication test hypotheses. Form (1985)

11. The authors concede that the self-employed might invest in education and training as a hedge against a future possibility that they may become wage and salary workers.

12. As the authors note, professional workers—in this case mainly doctors and lawyers—are extensively screened. See the discussion of occupational licensing, a form of screening between the provider of professional and skilled services and their clientele, in chapter 5.

compared the earnings of the self-employed and wage earners in a multiple-regression equation in an effort to establish the social class of the self-employed. The earnings model included human capital variables—education, vocational training, work experience, and skill level—as well as social and demographic characteristics, including gender, race, and marital and labor force statuses. In general, the results yielded few statistically significant differences between the self-employed and wage and salary workers which would account for their respective earnings. The self-employed benefited more from vocational training and less from skill and weeks worked during the census year.

Brock, Evans, and Phillips (1986) also approached the earnings issue eclectically, by including both social and demographic variables such as age, race, nativity, occupation, and urban location, as well as human capital variables, such as education and military experience. Significant positive differences in favor of the self-employed were found for urban location, college graduation, and military service since the Vietnam War. Negative differences favoring wage workers turned up for management, sales, and craft occupations. For self-employed workers alone, urban location, time elapsed since immigration, college graduation, and a combined age-education variable increased earnings, while immigrant status had a negative impact. Without further discussion of the expected effects, no strong conclusion can be drawn from the results of this study.

As noted previously, in his study of the growth of nonfarm self-employment, Blau (1987) utilized the same model to explain both the change in employment and the change in earnings. The earnings model in this study may be characterized as hedonistic; that is, both wage workers and the self-employed responded to changes in relative earnings in an effort to maximize utility. Thus, except for age and a variable representing structural change in the economy, marginal tax rates, social insurance benefits, and the statutory minimum wage constitute the model. Other variables, such as managerial ability, could not be measured but were implied. In some respects, the predictions of the model were confirmed. As self-employment expanded in the industries in which it is more common, the earnings of the self-employed fell relative to those of wage and salary workers in the economy as a whole. An earnings regression for those dependent only on self-employment found a weak positive response to the lower of two marginal rates of income tax. None of the other variables were statistically significant. Although the R^2 reported is substantially higher in this than in any of the other studies reviewed, such findings would not seem to advance understanding of the earnings of the self-employed very far.[13]

Summary and Conclusions

Although qualified by some problems of measurement, especially the underreporting of income and earnings by the self-employed, the data reviewed in this chapter demonstrate that on average the return to labor among self-employed workers falls below that of ostensibly comparable wage and salary workers. While this was shown to be a recent development, the precise dating of the decline from an earnings advantage for the self-employed in the early postwar years could not be firmly established. Of the factors believed to have contributed to the unfavorable earnings of the self-employed, few if any distinguished the self-employed from more highly paid wage and salary workers.

Five studies that included an analysis of self-employment earnings were reviewed. Differences in approach and context may account in part for their failure to achieve a consensus on the major factors contributing to the earnings differential between the two classes of employment. In general, too, there were fewer explanations for earnings variations for the self-employed than for wage and salary workers.

Some of these studies suggest that individuals with less competitive market characteristics tend to sort themselves into self-employment. The market characteristics of new entrants during the recent period of growth may differ particularly from those of earlier cohorts, thus accounting to some degree for the decline in earnings advantage. Changes in the structure of job opportunities, especially in the industrial and occupational dimensions of self-employment, may also be a promising area of investigation. If opportunities for self-employment have been growing in the lower-paying strata of industries and occupation, while opportunities for wage and salary workers have been in higher-paid substrata, the present earnings differential could have been the result. As in many similar cases, however, it is unlikely that any single factor will be found to be the key. In chapter 6, both the findings and the questions raised in this chapter will be incorporated into a proposed agenda for additional research on self-employment.

---

13. In all of the other studies substantially less than half the variance was explained in a statistical sense. Where separate regressions were run for the self-employed and wage workers, the unexplained fraction of earnings variability was consistently greater for the self-employed.

CHAPTER FOUR

Social and Cultural Structure of Self-Employment

Nonfarm self-employment is not a mirror image of the U.S. labor force. Although changes in the demographic and social composition of the self-employed during the 1970s and 1980s tended to move that group toward convergence with wage and salary workers, significantly large differences remain between the two groups. Compared with their representation in wage and salary employment, women, racial and ethnic minorities, and the foreign-born are underrepresented in nonfarm self-employment. Self-employment tends to be more common among retirement-age workers, newly arrived immigrants, the working poor, and workers in certain professional and skilled manual occupations. Consideration of the role of self-employment among these various groups should help us understand recent developments in self-employment. In most instances, however, additional and more penetrating research is needed.

Self-Employed Women

Women undoubtedly have made the largest contribution of any group to the demographic and social changes in the composition of the self-employed during the post–World War II period. But compared with all women in nonfarm employment, women in self-employment are underrepresented. This has occurred despite a markedly higher increase in the proportion of women in self-employment than in nonfarm employment. Furthermore, the average earnings of self-employed women are well below the average of women in wage and salary jobs, as well as those of men in both wage and salary jobs and self-employment, and this gap has widened over time.

TABLE 4.1. NONFARM EMPLOYMENT, BY CLASS OF WORKER AND GENDER, 1987 (in thousands)

Class of worker	Total	Male	Female	% female
Total employed	108,972	59,525	49,447	45.4
Wage and salary	100,771	54,102	46,669	46.3
Self-employed	8,201	5,423	2,778	33.9
% self-employed	8.4	9.1	5.6	

SOURCE: SBA 1988.

Almost 3 million women were engaged in nonfarm self-employment in 1987. Overall, they accounted for one-third of nonfarm self-employment, compared with 45 percent of all nonfarm employment (table 4.1). In addition, there was a sharp and relatively persistent difference in the percentage of men and women who were self-employed. While nearly 10 percent of men were self-employed, less than 6 percent of women were so engaged.

Men still constitute a majority of the nonfarm self-employed. As noted in chapter 1, however, women have been entering self-employment and small business at exceptionally rapid rates. Becker (1984) reported that in the period 1970–83 women were entering self-employment at rates five times greater than that of men and three times greater than that of women into wage and salary jobs. Data prepared by the Small Business Administration for a similar period, 1972–85, indicates an annual rate of increase among women of 5.1 percent compared with an overall annual increase in self-employment of 2.9 percent. During that period almost exactly half of the total gain in nonfarm self-employment was accounted for by the entry of women across a broad spectrum of industries. Bureau of Labor Statistics data for the period 1980–87 show that the increase in self-employment among women was three times greater than among men (SBA 1988).

INDUSTRIAL AND OCCUPATIONAL TRENDS

Recent popular accounts have made much of the emergence and growth of entrepreneurship among women, often focusing on their entry into so-called nontraditional fields. But although gains were registered in every major nonfarm industry during the period 1972–85, there were marked variations among industries (table 4.2). In relative terms, the largest gains were in industries in which the participation of self-employed women in 1972 was relatively low, such as manufacturing, mining, construction, and wholesale

TABLE 4.2. SELF-EMPLOYED WOMEN IN NONFARM INDUSTRIES, 1972 AND 1985 (in thousands)

	1972		1985	
Industry	All self-employed[a]	% women	All self-employed[a]	% women
All industries	5,365	25.6	7,810	33.3
Mining	13	—[b]	20	5.0
Construction	746	1.3	1,301	4.4
Manufacturing	244	9.0	347	25.4
Transport and utilities	203	5.9	315	13.3
Wholesale trade	213	6.6	305	16.7
Retail trade	1,475	30.1	1,487	44.3
Finance, etc.	262	19.0	558	33.3
Services	2,209	37.0	3,477	43.8
Private household	30	96.7	6	16.7
Business and repair	488	11.3	1,185	27.8
Personal	730	65.6	882	76.0
Education and recreation	98	27.5	165	31.5
Professional	841	27.1	1,199	38.9

SOURCES: 1972, U.S. Department of Labor 1988; 1985, U.S. Department of Labor, *Employment and Earnings,* January 1986.
[a]Excludes incorporated self-employed.
[b]Less than .01 percent.

trade. By contrast, in retail trade, where the share of women in self-employment was relatively high in both years, the gain was less than 1 percent. And, not surprisingly, only modest gains were made in the nongoods services,[1] where the share of women in self-employment was above the average for the industry in 1972. In broad terms, in fact, there was relatively little change in the industrial distribution of self-employed women. In 1972, the nongoods services accounted for 41 percent of nonfarm self-employment among women; in 1985, the same group of industries accounted for only slightly more, 44 percent.

If trade, finance, insurance, and real estate are included in a broader category of service industries, there was virtually no change between the two years in the industrial location of women in self-employment. In both 1972 and 1985, services accounted for 59 percent of such employment. In-

1. Nongoods services include business and repair services, education and recreation, professional services, and so on, as distinct from wholesale and retail trade, finance, and insurance, where physical products are the principal items of exchange.

ternal Revenue Service data for a more recent period, 1980–85, show that the fraction of service industry sole proprietorships owned by women dropped only 2 points, from 95 to 93 percent.[2] More detailed employment data might indicate a greater degree of change in the industrial location of self-employed women. Thus far, however, the data do not seem to support this perception.

The participation of women in self-employment has increased in Western Europe as well as in the United States. The OECD reports that between 1969 and 1986 the proportion of self-employed women in nonfarm employment increased from 24.1 percent to 28.4 percent in its sixteen member countries taken together. This increase was not uniform across individual countries, however. In the Mediterranean countries, notably Italy, self-employment among women appears to have declined during the period (OECD 1986).

Developments in the United Kingdom, one of the few countries that for reasons of public policy has closely monitored self-employment,[3] have closely paralleled those in the United States. Between 1972 and 1988, total self-employment increased by nearly 50 pecent, in sharp contrast to total employment, which grew by just over 4 percent (*Employment Gazette,* 1989). Again, as in the United States, self-employed women have led this growth, accounting for a third of the increase. Over the sixteen-year period, the number of British women who were self-employed increased by 79 percent, twice that of men. In 1988, one of every four self-employed persons was a woman.

In this case again, at least in broad terms, the rate of entry of self-employed women into nontraditional employment is not unusual. Small numbers at the beginning of the period give the illusion of major breakthroughs. In construction, for example, between 1971 and 1988, there was an eightfold increase in the numbers of self-employed women, but in the latter year women still constituted only 6 percent of the self-employed in that industry. In broad sectors also, the industrial distribution of self-employed women and men in 1988 was similar to that of the United States. Although a majority of both men and women were employed in services, 86 percent of self-employed women worked in this sector compared with 54 percent of self-employed men.

---

2. Calculated from data in SBA 1988.
3. See the discussion in chapter 5.

TABLE 4.3. SELF-EMPLOYMENT AS A PERCENTAGE OF WOMEN IN SELECTED OCCUPATIONS, 1970 AND 1980[a]

Occupation	1970	1980
Accountants	5.5%	3.2%
Architects	2.5	20.7
Health-diagnosing occupations[b]	27.7	20.0
Lawyers[c]	34.6	14.9
Managers	18.4	9.2
Sales occupations	6.4	7.3
Precision crafts	6.2	6.7
Construction trades	14.3	15.9
Mechanical, metalworking	0.7	3.8
Services (except private household)	5.7	5.5
Personal	24.7	22.3

SOURCES: U.S. Bureau of the Census 1973, 1984c.
[a]Excludes incorporated self-employed.
[b]Doctors and dentists.
[c]Includes judges.

Census data (table 4.3) on rates of self-employment of women in a number of occupations in 1970 and 1980 show that although women have made substantial gains in certain fields, such as the health-diagnosing occupations and the practice of law, they appear to have entered these areas as salaried employees or wage earners rather than as self-employed workers. Only a few occupations are exceptions: architecture, among the professional occupations, and the precision crafts in construction and the metalworking trades. As in other cases, however, despite relative gains, the numbers of self-employed women in these occupations were small in both years.

In Britain, too, gender differences in the occupational pattern of self-employment are comparatively sharp. In 1984, 44 percent of self-employed women worked in managerial occupations, compared with 29 percent of self-employed men (Creigh, Roberts, et al. 1986). Eleven percent of the women were engaged in such personal services as cleaning and hairdressing, occupations that accounted for only 2 percent of self-employed men. By contrast, men were more likely to be employed in goods production or processing. Thirteen percent of self-employed men worked in construction, for example, compared with less than 1 percent of self-employed women.

A variety of factors reflecting broad changes in the structure of the economy as well as developments more specific to certain occupations and industries probably influenced the changes in the occupational pattern of self-employed women. Among these factors are changes in the organizational size and form in which services are delivered and the effects of taxation and regulation on the legal form of organization. Incorporation has been common in the professions and in some managerial occupations because of its tax advantages and protection against liability lawsuits, as well as its technical and economic advantages. Although we have no precise current information on the occupational composition of the incorporated self-employed, it is probable that Census data on self-employment (table 4.3) understate the number of self-employed workers and thus overstate the degree to which the self-employment of women in some occupations has declined.

As the industry and occupation data suggest, the large influx of women into self-employment in both the United States and Britain has not substantially changed patterns in the differences between the genders. The persistence of these differences is consistent with the marked earnings differences between self-employed men and women. An examination of earnings differences, then, may provide some clues to the differences in employment patterns. Women who choose self-employment over more highly paid wage and salary jobs, especially if opportunities in so-called nontraditional occupations are increasing, should exhibit particular labor market characteristics and behaviors.

EARNINGS

There appears to be little difference between the motives of men and women in choosing self-employment. Data on new entrants to self-employment in Great Britain show that independence and expected monetary rewards ranked about the same for men and women (Hakim 1989). Women were slightly more interested in the challenge of having their own business and were much more interested in having greater control over their time and labor. Nevertheless, they fared poorly in monetary terms compared with other groups.

Every usable source of data confirms that self-employed women earn significantly less than self-employed men and that their earnings are also considerably lower than those of both women and men in wage and salary jobs. The unfavorable earnings position of self-employed women, moreover, is not unique to the United States but is found to varying degrees in other industrialized countries.

TABLE 4.4. MEAN ANNUAL INCOME OF FULL-TIME, FULL-YEAR WORKERS, BY GENDER AND CLASS OF WORKER, 1974–1984[a]

| | Self-employed | | Wage and salary | | Self-employed/ |
Year	Men	Women as % of men	Men	Women as % of men	wage and salary (women)
1974	$8,834	27.8	$9,698	44.6	.57
1975	9,072	26.9	10,315	46.1	.52
1976	9,475	27.8	11,081	46.4	.51
1977	10,185	29.6	11,995	46.3	.54
1978	11,816	29.5	13,151	46.6	.57
1979	12,450	28.0	14,522	47.4	.51
1980	12,434	27.8	14,455	47.6	.50
1981	12,921	33.3	16,875	49.8	.51
1982	12,828	35.8	17,770	51.2	.52
1983	14,490	35.3	18,490	53.2	.52
1984	15,155	36.7	19,737	53.2	.53

SOURCE: SBA, *State of Small Business, 1986*, based on Current Population Survey, P-60 series, including unpublished data for 1984.
[a]Includes nonlabor income.

According to a study based on the new Survey of Income and Program Participation, in 1983 the annualized median earnings of women sole proprietors working full time were only 30 percent of those of similarly employed men (Haber, Lamas, and Lichtenstein 1987). Women in paid employment, by contrast, earned 60 percent of the median earnings of men in paid employment. Self-employed men, according to the same source, earned 60 percent of the earnings of men in paid employment, while self-employed women earned only 30 percent as much as women in wage jobs. The authors report, however, that these differences may be somewhat exaggerated because of a tendency among the self-employed to underreport their earnings.

Table 4.4 confirms the above results. Based on sample data from the Current Population Survey, it represents only full-time, full-year workers, thus controlling for one important factor in earnings differentials. The incomes reported include nonlabor as well as labor income; in both classes of employment, however, labor income generally accounts for well over 90 percent of the total reported. Both classes of employed women improved their earnings relative to men in the ten-year period 1974–84 and by approximately the same percentage point gain. The ratio of the earnings of

TABLE 4.5. FIVE-YEAR AVERAGES OF MEDIAN ANNUAL EARNINGS, BY
GENDER AND CLASS OF WORKER

Period	All wage and salary			Self-employed			Self-employed/ wage and salary (women)
	Men	Women	Women as % men	Men	Women	Women as % men	
1955–59	$3,565	$1,511	42	$2,837	$1,626	57	1.08
1960–64	4,119	1,803	44	3,456	1,749	51	.97
1965–69	5,239	2,264	43	5,004	2,142	43	.94
1970–74	6,905	3,068	44	6,702	2,605	39	.85
1975–79	11,206	4,490	40	9,006	3,403	38	.76
1980–84	13,632	7,230	53	10,699	4,500	42	.62

SOURCE: U.S. Department of Health and Human Services 1989.

self-employed women to the earnings of women in paid employment, however, showed virtually no improvement.

In the prewar and early post–World War II period, the relative earnings
position of self-employed women was much more favorable than in recent years. Although their data source is probably not representative of all
self-employed women at that time, Elliott and Manson (1930) reported
in a study of fourteen thousand business and professional women that
independently-employed women earned "considerably more" than salaried
women in their sample. In 1927, for example, the median annual earnings
of the salaried respondents were $1,540, compared with $2,043 for the
independently employed. The reported earnings did not include income
earned outside their principal occupations. Independent women, not surprisingly, had a very different occupational mix than women in paid employment, with much larger proportions in the then nontraditional fields of law,
finance, and editorial work. Salaried women were more likely to be employed in clerical and secretarial jobs. Also, 27 percent of the independents
had some higher education, compared with only 2 percent of the salaried
women.

Social Security earnings data (table 4.5) suggest a deterioration in the
relative earnings position of self-employed women during the period 1955–
84. Because these data do not distinguish full-time, full-year workers from
others, the influence of differences in time worked cannot be taken into
account. Nonetheless, women in paid employment seem to be holding their
own in comparison with similarly employed men, while self-employed
women experienced a drop in earnings relative to both self-employed

TABLE 4.6. RATIO OF MEDIAN ANNUAL EARNINGS OF WOMEN EMPLOYED YEAR ROUND, FULL-TIME TO MEN'S EARNINGS, BY OCCUPATION AND CLASS OF WORKER, 1982

Occupation	Wage and salary	Self-employed
All occupations	.62	.46
Managerial and professional	.63	.42
Technical, sales, administrative support	.59	.47
Services	.63	.44
Craft occupations	.65	.54
Operatives and laborers	.64	.49

SOURCE: Adapted from Becker 1984.

men and women in wage and salary jobs. One might speculate that the relative decline in the earnings of self-employed women is the result of a movement into lower-paying or part-time work or an increase in the proportion of self-employed women with limited or poorer quality human capital characteristics.

Explaining the lower earnings of women in self-employment compared to their wage and salary counterparts becomes more difficult when not only time devoted to work but the occupation and legal form of organization are taken into account. Data from Becker (1984) show that compared with their male counterparts in each broad occupational group, the earnings of women working full time, year round in wage and salary jobs are on average almost one-third higher than those of comparable self-employed women (table 4.6).

As noted earlier, the incorporated self-employed are generally located in higher-paying occupations and may, as in the case of managers of small businesses, employ others. Both of these factors tend to make their earnings higher than those of individuals who are dependent solely on their own efforts and skills and who do not receive the tax and other advantages of incorporation. Thus the inclusion of the incorporated self-employed in measuring earnings has a significant effect. The median earnings of unincorporated self-employed men were 73 percent of those of men engaged solely in paid employment. When the incorporated self-employed were added, however, the median annual earnings were *higher* than those of wage and salary workers by a little more than 1 percent (SBA, *State of Small Business, 1986*). Unincorporated self-employed women earned 59 percent as much as employed women; for all self-employed women, this figure increased, but only to 79 percent of the earnings of women in paid employment. Thus incorporation for self-employed women was not as advantageous as it was for self-employed men.

Internal Revenue Service data suggest that in recent years the earnings of women in small businesses may be improving relative to those of men. Data prepared by that agency for the SBA for the period 1980–85 show that total business receipts of female sole proprietors increased by 38 percent in 1982 dollars, compared with a gain of only a little more than 1 percent for all nonfarm businesses (SBA 1988). Above-average gains were recorded in all but two industry groups—finance, insurance, and real estate and whole-sale and retail trade. Still, in 1985, the average receipts of women propri-etors in constant dollars were only 35 percent of those of male proprietors in nonfarm industries.

WHY EARNINGS OF SELF-EMPLOYED WOMEN ARE LOW

Few studies have considered the earnings and employment of self-employed women, and only one has made them a central concern. This is probably in part the result of a failure to recognize the importance of the recent increase in self-employment among women and the inadequacy of the data bases for in-depth analysis. One recent study built on a proposal by this author and augmented by additional methodological considerations (Little 1990) represents a promising start in this area. Absent further supporting evi-dence, however, the factors underlying the high rates of growth and the relatively low earnings of self-employed women are treated in this section as hypotheses.

One factor that undoubtedly has increased the self-employment rates of women is the general growth of women's participation in the labor force. In the past few decades participation rates have not only approached those of men but, more important for our purposes, have become more stable, even among married women with school-age children performing the multiple roles of spouse, mother, and contributor to household money income. Sta-bilization implies both a qualitative and a quantitative increase in human capital through on-the-job training and experience in so-called traditional and nontraditional jobs. Larger investments in human capital, especially through experience, seem to be associated with the propensity for choosing self-employment, as suggested by the above-average age of both self-employed men and women. Since the levels of formal educational attain-ment do not differ much between women who are employees and those who are self-employed, differences in labor force continuity and experience may be involved in the growth of self-employment among women.

As suggested by Little (1990), understanding the participation rate and earnings of self-employed women depends on the ability to analyze these relationships within the framework of the family or household. In most published sources, this capability does not exist. Little suggests, as one line of inquiry, examining the degree to which the increase in women's labor force participation rate, especially the growth of the two-earner family, has created opportunities for self-employment. The shift from household to market production implied in the increase in the labor force participation rate may have generated opportunities for self-employment by a substitution effect (i.e., market goods and services replaced household-produced goods and services).[4]

Although earnings and employment comparisons between employed and self-employed women are, with the exception discussed below, lacking, some useful comparisons of male and female business owners are available from a study commissioned by the SBA on business ownership.[5] Compared with nonminority male sole proprietors, female sole proprietors in 1982 were younger and more likely to be married. They had among them a higher proportion of high school graduates, and a slightly smaller proportion had four or more years of college. In addition, women sole proprietors as a group have fewer years of experience as employees before becoming self-employed and a smaller proportion have prior experience as business owners. Although some of these differences—age, marital status, and education, for example—are cohort effects, they suggest that the relatively lower earnings of women compared with men in self-employment may reflect relatively smaller human capital endowments. Women choosing self-employment would, on this assumption, be sorting themselves into jobs congruent with their productivity characteristics.

The shift in the industrial structure of employment from the goods to the service industries sector may have influenced the growth of self-employment among women, but it is not itself the sole cause. As noted earlier, the service industries have long accounted for the majority of self-employed women. The sector experienced relatively rapid growth, however,

---

4. Such a phenomenon, if true, must be in activities other than domestic service, since that is one of the occupations in which self-employment has experienced a sharp decrease in the postwar decades.

5. U.S. Bureau of the Census 1987. The data gathered in this survey are summarized in SBA 1988, chaps. 4 and 5.

well before the increase in self-employment among women in the mid-1970s and thus cannot independently have accounted for this increase.

Developments within the service industries that may have facilitated the entry of women have yet to be explored. Technological innovation, especially in electronic communication and the computerization of clerical and secretarial work, enabling women with school-age children, for example, to work at home and reduce work-related expenses such as transportation, clothing, and child care, could have contributed to their choosing self-employment. In such cases, the after-tax net earnings in real terms might be greater than the earnings in paid employment.

EARNINGS COMPARISONS

In an attempt to explain gender differences in the earnings of the self-employed, Little (1990) tested the effect of human capital and other variables on a sample of officers and enlisted personnel in the military reserves, selected from among those who had civilian jobs and those who were self-employed.[6] Separate regressions for gender and class of worker and regressions in which class of work was interacted with the variables in the model, including education and experience, were run. The model was also tested on measures of weekly earnings and annual income. In the separate regressions, there was virtually no distinction between the two classes of employed women on these human capital variables. For both groups the returns from education and experience were positive and statistically significant. Compared with male employees in the interactive analysis, education had a negative influence on the earnings and income of both classes of women workers. Experience was not statistically significant for either group.

As Little and others have pointed out, self-employment provides a wider range of choice between market work and home production devoted, for example, to housekeeping and childrearing. Thus women who provide market goods and services while working in their homes may be compensated for lower money earnings by the increase in utility derived from being able to devote more time to child rearing and homemaking, as well as by the reduction in work expenses. There is, however, little research bearing on

---

6. The author is careful to point out that the sample is not representative of the general working-age population since relatively few women have been in the military reserves and, because of military retirement policy, reservists tend to be younger than the civilian labor force as a whole.

this hypothesis. Hakim (1989) reported that a survey in Great Britain found that 78 percent of all self-employment was home-based. Men were more likely than women to perform their work away from their residences, while women were more likely to work at home. A study of entry into self-employment based on employment histories in West Germany found the proportion of women in family-based enterprises to be more than twice the proportion of women in other forms of self-employment (Carroll and Mosakowski 1987). In that study, too, earnings were negatively related to the proportion of women in self employment.

Evans and Leighton (1987) included children under age three as an independent variable in their estimation of the probability of self-employment. This variable turned out to be positive and statistically significant only for women with postgraduate education who had incorporated their enterprises—hardly representative of self-employed women as a whole.

Little (1990) included dependents (presumably mostly children) and employed spouses in his earnings model. Although the sign of the coefficient on dependents was negative, as anticipated, it neither distinguished self-employed women nor was statistically significant. Statistically, having an employed spouse had no effect on the earnings of either class of women workers. It is perhaps significant that in this study and others that deal with gender differences in earnings, the models offer limited insight into the earnings of women compared with those of men, regardless of the type of employment.

Several authors suggest that consumer discrimination may be in part responsible for the unfavorable earnings position of self-employed women (Sanborn 1964; Fuchs 1971; Oaxaca 1973; Brown 1976). This hypothesis, at least until tested, appears implausible, for at least two reasons. First, a substantial fraction of goods and services produced by women are purchased by women, either for themselves or for their households. Second, this discrimination ought to affect women in wage and salary jobs as well. Profit-maximizing employers in firms and industries marked by high levels of direct consumer contact would be expected to resist employing women if discrimination had a negative effect on sales and revenues. But not only are the proportions of women employees in such industries equal to or greater than the all-industry average, but relative to the self-employed they also enjoy higher earnings. The only study that has considered the influence of consumer discrimination on self-employment and its earnings deals with racial minorities (Borjas and Bronars 1989), which will be discussed later in this chapter. The arguments of that study have little bearing on the issue of the earnings of self-employed women.

STRUCTURAL AND BEHAVIORAL FACTORS

More plausible explanations for the lower earnings of self-employed women must include both structural and behavioral differences between the self-employed and wage and salary workers. These include gender differences in industrial and occupational distributions, the scale and capitalization of businesses owned by women, women's attitudes toward economic risk, and their degree of commitment to and/or dependence on self-employment.

In chapter 2, I noted a marked difference in the industrial and occupational employment distributions between men and women. Regardless of the type of employment, a disproportionate number of women tend to be found in the lower-paying industrial sectors and in the lower-paying occupations within most of those sectors. Trade and service establishments provide employment for a majority of women, most of whom are in the semiskilled and less-skilled occupations. The pattern for self-employed men and women is similar to the overall employment pattern in the United States and elsewhere.[7]

The real puzzle is that while the industrial and occupational employment distributions of self-employed women are similar to those of women in paid employment, at least in the broad categories, their earnings are dramatically lower. As noted earlier in this chapter, for full-time, full-year workers the earnings of self-employed women in 1983 were less than one-third of those of women employees. A finer breakdown of the industrial and occupational distributions might reveal the significance of these factors, but published sources restrict such an analysis.

Differences in the earnings of the self-employed may be accounted for in part by degree of commitment as reflected in time worked. While this measure helps to explain the earnings difference between self-employed men and women, it does not clarify the earnings differences between women in self-employment and women in wage and salary jobs. According to the Survey of Income and Program Participation, 73 percent of male nonfarm business owners worked full time in their businesses, compared with 44 percent of female business owners (Haber, Lamas, and Lichtenstein 1987). One-third of women business owners were either casual or part-time owners, com-

---

7. Great Britain is similar, for example. See Creigh, Roberts, et al (1986).

pared with only a little more than one-fifth of men. Weeks worked per year in 1983 were virtually the same for salaried and self-employed women, but the proportion of the latter working more than forty hours per week was nearly three times larger (SBA, *State of Small Business, 1986*).[8] Once more, there is an anomaly: self-employed women in full-year jobs work longer hours but have substantially lower earnings than their salaried counterparts in similar industrial and occupational settings.

One plausible explanation for the low and declining relative earnings of self-employed women is the relatively lower scale and level of capitalization of their business enterprises. A higher proportion of businesses owned by women are home-based[9] and their receipts are substantially lower than those of men. The average business receipts of women sole proprietors in 1983 were only about one-third those of men, despite the previous growth of self-employment among women. In combination with the gender differences in industrial and occupational distribution, these observations imply a much smaller scale of enterprise among self-employed women.[10]

A 1982 survey of business owners (SBA 1988) provides substantial support for the importance of the role of business capital in explaining gender differences in earnings. On average, women sole proprietors started their businesses with only half the capital of men and were less likely than nonminority men to have borrowed the capital, partly because a larger proportion of women reported that no capital was required.[11]

The relatively low levels of capitalization of enterprises owned by women may result from a variety of institutional factors, for example, access to business finance. A federal interagency task force report on women business owners in a study prepared by the U.S. Treasury (1978) based on a six-city survey showed that women business owners were more likely than men to rely on so-called angel money—personal savings and loans from

---

8. Although not tied to earnings differences, the work time differences are very similar in Britain. In 1984, one-third of self-employed women worked more than forty hours per week, compared with only 12 percent of women in paid employment (Creigh, Roberts, et al. 1986).

9. An Internal Revenue Service study (Grayson 1982) reported that women sole proprietors were 10 percent more likely than men to report the same address for both residence and place of business.

10. There are exceptions, of course. In construction and transportation and communication, in 1983, the receipts of women sole proprietors exceeded those of men in those industries. But women accounted, respectively, for only 4 and 8 percent of the enterprises in those industries (SBA, *State of Small Business, 1986*).

11. In the original survey, 39 percent of women sole proprietors required no capital, compared with 27 percent of men proprietors. In terms of self-financing, however, only slightly more men than women relied on that source rather than on borrowing.

friends and relatives. Two-thirds of the women surveyed financed their enterprises with such sources, while men were more likely to seek funding from commercial banks and other formal lending institutions. The same study reported that, at that time, there were almost no government programs designed to prepare women for business ownership,[12] nor were financial institutions making any special efforts to develop women business owners as clientele.

A more recent study prepared for the SBA in 1985 indicates that while dependence on personal sources of finance is still more common among women than among men, it may be prevalent mainly among start-up or first-time business owners. Once a business is established, according to the study, the sources of finance are virtually the same for men and women (SBA 1986). A survey of about three thousand women business owners in ten European countries (Commission of the European Communities 1987) found that about 80 percent of the married women business owners— roughly three-fifths of the sample—reported that they could negotiate bank loans without a cosigner. The survey did not report the proportion of women who began their businesses with such loans.

The issue of discrimination by financial institutions against women business owners remains moot. One way of posing the question is, Do women choose lower-paying businesses because they are unable to obtain financing for larger-scale and higher-paying enterprises, or is the level of financing obtainable, especially from financial institutions, generally lower than that for men because of a propensity among women to establish smaller-scale and financially riskier enterprises?

The 1978 task force report leans toward the latter conclusion; however, sorting out the underlying forces that would support this conclusion is not easy. Following certain explanations for earnings differences between men and women summarized in Blau and Ferber (1986), it might be argued that women choose to establish enterprises that minimize the adverse impact on their human and financial capital of such career interruptions as raising a family. The small scale of the enterprises, on the one hand, and the reluctance of banks to lend to a perceived high-risk borrower, on the other, would be consistent with such a hypothesis. One study reports that, compared with self-employed men, the median tenure of women in self-

---

12. The SBA has conducted free workshops on starting one's own business, but these are not specially targeted to women. There have been several private nonprofit organizations, however, that have specialized in helping women become business owners. For a brief account of their programs, see Lawson 1985.

employment in 1981 was only half as great as that of all employed women (Horvath 1983); this statistic does not take into account the recent increase in self-employed women, however, or the age-cohort differences in job tenure among men and women.

At present, women business owners and financial institutions may each be limited by their perceptions of the risks involved. For the situation to change, women may need to improve their preparation for and change their thinking about business ownership. Financial institutions, for their part, may have to support more strongly women who plan to embark on larger-scale and longer careers in business ownership.

The puzzle of the relatively low earnings of self-employed women in the United States is compounded by the more favorable earnings position of self-employed women in other countries. According to OECD data, self-employed women in the United States earned only 25 percent as much as self-employed men. In eleven other countries in the early 1980s, the earnings ratios for self-employed women to men were all substantially higher and even approached parity in Australia (86.6 percent) and Sweden (71.8 percent). In all the other countries the earnings ratio was at least twice that of the United States (OECD 1986). In most of these countries, moreover, the percentage of self-employed women reaching the top decile of the distribution of men's earnings was, on average, three times greater than that in the United States. The European survey (Commission of the European Communities 1987) found that about 80 percent of women business owners felt they were at no disadvantage compared with men in similar lines of self-employment. They believed that their remuneration, including income, was about the same. Despite this sense of equality, self-employed women were unhappy with their low earnings.[13] In addition, they complained of the absence of a "normal family life," mainly because of their long working hours. Clearly, explaining the increase in self-employment among women as it relates to their earnings position is complex and yet to be well understood.

Race and the Self-Employed

Historically, self-employment and small business ownership have been an important path by which ethnic, racial, and religious minorities in the

---

13. There is no necessary inconsistency in these findings. Although the report does not so indicate, the self-employed women could at the same time accept the fairness of their earnings and regret the low-paid employments in which they were engaged.

United States have overcome social and cultural disabilities and entered the so-called mainstream. Ethnic and racial minorities have been part of the recent increase in self-employment, usually at rates in excess of the overall rate of growth. According to SBA data (*State of Small Business, 1986*), nonwhite self-employment in nonfarm industries grew by 64 percent between 1975 and 1985, almost twice the overall rate of employment growth.

Despite this recent increase, however, the self-employment rate remains relatively low and is quite uneven among minority groups. As a percentage of the civilian labor force, the self-employment rate of native-born whites increased from 5.7 in 1975 to 6.3 in 1985. The self-employment rate of nonwhites increased from .03 percent to .05 percent during that period. Increases among Asian-Americans have been close to those of native whites, but in 1980 the self-employment rates of Hispanics and blacks relative to total nonfarm employment were only 3.8 and 2.4 percent, respectively. A study of males from twenty-five to sixty-four years of age based on 1980 census data reports the same relative ranking of the self-employment rates of these racial groups (Borjas and Bronars 1989). The relative rates do not appear to have changed much since then (SBA, *State of Small Business, 1986*).[14]

Taken as a whole, the industrial distribution of minority self-employment differs only marginally from the pattern of native whites. In 1981, nonwhite self-employment was proportionally slightly greater than white self-employment in retail trade and personal services, especially in educational and recreation services and nonhospital medical and health services. During the period of accelerated growth of self-employment, 1972–81, nonwhites registered above-average gains in wholesale trade, finance and insurance, and business and repair services—industries in which their previous participation had been exceptionally low (U.S. Department of Labor 1982).

Despite their relatively low self-employment rates, blacks have made significant gains in small business ownership, predominantly as self-employed entrepreneurs. Two surveys of minority-owned enterprises, in 1977 and 1982, show an overall increase of 47 percent. Retail trade and the various services together accounted for more than two-thirds of this increase (SBA, *State of Small Business, 1986*).

Published data on the occupational distribution of self-employment according to ethnic and racial characteristics are not available. Without providing

---

14. The recent boycott by blacks against Korean greengrocers located in black neighborhoods in New York City has dramatized these differences. Some blacks, however, have followed the Korean example by opening their own fruit stands (Roberts 1990).

TABLE 4.7. SOLE PROPRIETORSHIPS AND BUSINESS RECEIPTS, BY MINORITY GROUP STATUS, 1982

	No. of firms	%	Receipts	%	Average receipts
All minorities	792,509	100	$25,308,836	100	$31,935
Blacks	322,975	41	6,583,241	26	20,383
Hispanics	233,476	29	8,422,488	33	36,074
Asian-Americans, Native Americans, Alaskan natives	236,058	30	10,303,107	41	43,646

SOURCE: U.S. Bureau of the Census 1984–85.

detail, Becker (1984) reported that white self-employed workers were more likely than similarly employed black workers to be in managerial, professional, and technical occupations. Self-employed blacks were more heavily engaged in manual occupations. No comparable information was provided on other ethnic or racial groups.

The earnings of minority self-employed workers are generally much lower than those of their native white counterparts and vary considerably across racial groups. Borjas and Bronars's (1989) data on prime working-age males show mean self-employment incomes among blacks in 1980 to have been about 47 percent less than those of self-employed whites. The incomes of self-employed Hispanics were 28 percent less than, while those of self-employed Asians were nearly equal to, those of whites. In 1982, average receipts of sole proprietorships owned by blacks were $19,800, compared with about $42,000 for all nonfarm sole proprietorships. Business receipts as a proxy for self-employment incomes also suggest significant earnings differences across nonwhite racial groups. Although the proportion of minority-owned businesses differs little across racial groups—about 95 percent in each group are individual proprietorships—both the shares of total business receipts for all groups and the average receipts of individual proprietorships differ considerably (table 4.7). In 1982, though black proprietors accounted for the single largest number and proportion of individual proprietorships, their share of both total business receipts and average receipts accounted for by all minority proprietors were the lowest of the three groups. Asian-Americans and a scattering of Native Americans and Alaskan Natives, by contrast, enjoyed larger average receipts and the largest share of all minority proprietors.

The low earnings and low participation rate of blacks in small business, despite some recent gains and support under government programs, discussed in chapter 5, are puzzling. On the face of the matter, compared with recent cohorts of foreign-born ethnic and racial minorities,[15] blacks would seem to have several advantages. Unfamiliarity with the language and with social and economic institutions should not be a problem for blacks, as they might be for newly arrived immigrants.[16] Further, the concentration in urban areas of the black American population would seem to offer a high degree of potential patronage for economically viable businesses. Moreover, if self-employment offers a defense against discrimination, we might expect to see higher rates of self-employment among blacks than among other minorities.

There has been much theorizing and some limited empirical research directed toward understanding the low rate of self-employment among blacks. Both economic and sociocultural explanations have been offered. Some authors have suggested that low incomes, because they allow for limited personal savings, reduce the availability of the financial resources needed to start a small business. Light (1980) challenges this notion, pointing out that all ethnic minorities have had to contend with the same problem in financing their enterprises. Moreover, he states, rotating or cooperative credit institutions are part of the black cultural heritage, as in Nigeria. Lack of management training and technical experience, perhaps because of poor education, has been advanced as another possible reason (Mayers 1978; Doctors and Appel 1974). But if this is the case, why should wage and salary employment be a more attractive alternative? Poor education and training would imply low earnings for employees as well as the self-employed. Still another study argues that the black cultural heritage is communitarian and thus not oriented to capitalist motivation (Sonfield 1976); but Kotkin (1986) points to the relative economic success of West Indian immigrants, who share a similar social and cultural history.

DISCRIMINATION THEORY AND THE ENCLAVE HYPOTHESIS

Two other lines of argument that have been explored beyond anecdote and casual empiricism concern the roles of discrimination and a form of networking. Discrimination theory argues that if employers undervalue workers because of race or some other economically irrelevant characteristic,

---

15. Other ethnic and racial minorities are discussed below, since a majority are recent immigrants.

16. Evans (1989), however, speculates that sharing a common language and major cultural attributes with the majority white population may have discouraged black entrepreneurship in the United States. Based on his study of ethnic minorities in Australia, he concludes that a language barrier creates an isolated labor pool and thus a spur to self-employment in the ethnic community instead of wage employment in the mainstream economy.

they create an incentive for self-employment (Sowell 1981). Thus, whether because of consumer tastes and preferences or employer prejudice, black self-employed workers are displaced by discriminatory policies or practices into less desirable and lower-paying enterprises. It follows from this hypothesis that low earnings in self-employment produce limited resources for additional investment, larger-scale enterprises, or higher earnings, thus perpetuating the low-earnings pattern of black self-employment.

But again, why is this result necessary? The Myrdals' classic study (1944) argued that consumer discrimination by whites forced black entrepreneurs to trade mostly with other blacks, principally through personal service businesses such as barbershops, beauty salons, and funeral parlors, all small-scale enterprises requiring little capital for entry and, on average, yielding relatively low returns. Efforts to enter other lines of self-employment would meet not only discrimination by consumers but also the better-financed competition of white businesses.

Borjas and Bronars (1989) have tested the hypothesis of direct consumer discrimination in relation to the differential rates of self-employment among minority groups. They adapt the Becker-Arrow model of discrimination in labor markets to self-employment, arguing that because of imperfect information (i.e., prejudice), white or other nonblack consumers will purchase goods and services from black merchants only at prices sufficiently low to compensate them for the "disutility" of contact with blacks. Because of the lower returns in self-employment, a disproportionate number of blacks with higher ability choose to work in wage and salary jobs. Blacks with lower levels of ability, by contrast, will be more likely to be self-employed, with correspondingly lower earnings. The authors tested this model on men aged twenty-five to sixty-four in 1980, comparing both predicted and actual earnings differences between whites and blacks, Asians, and Hispanics. They found the earnings differentials consistent with the model's hypotheses, that blacks in self-employment have lower relative earnings than those in salaried jobs.

Approaching the issue from somewhat different perspectives, two other studies reach a similar conclusion. Bearse (1984), using data from the 1976 Survey of Income and Education, found that the main reason for low self-employment rates among black men was the high opportunity cost; given their human capital characteristics, black men experienced higher returns in wage and salary jobs. This study also found that black women had a propensity for self-employment but that their influence on self-employment earnings was quite low.

Thompson (1986) studied a sample of a little more than two thousand graduates of the member institutions of the United Negro Colleges in an effort to discover the pattern of their postgraduate careers. He found that 6 percent of the graduates (12 percent of the male and 3 percent of the female alumni) were self-employed, in insurance, accounting, medicine, law, and mortuary services. Forty-five percent of this group's clientele were predominantly black; only 2 percent served an all-white clientele. In terms of economic and social equality, black-owned businesses ranked lowest among all social and economic institutions. Forty-eight percent of the alumni sample considered business ownership an ineffective vehicle for upward mobility and integration into the mainstream economy.

The enclave hypothesis, which has been employed principally to understand differential rates of economic and social integration among recent immigrants, argues that groups tied by cultural and social characteristics will succeed to the degree to which there is a strong network of support among them. An enclave—that is, a high concentration of a particular ethnic group, often in a distinctive urban neighborhood—provides social and financial capital and a market for the goods and services of racial and ethnic enterprises. According to this hypothesis, relatively weak networks among blacks could explain their low rates of and low earnings in self-employment. The evidence, however, is not conclusive. Data from the 1982 Characteristics of Business Owners survey, summarized in the SBA's *Small Business in the American Economy* (1988), show black sole proprietors, compared with other minorities and male nonminority owners, to have the lowest proportions of relatives who own a business and of family and friends as sources of capital. Black businesses had the highest proportion of customers or clientele from their own minority group, however,[17] and among those businesses with employees, they hired the highest proportion of minority employees. The latter characteristics suggest a high degree of solidarity and support; other factors such as low incomes and savings may be exerting a negative influence on the growth and success of black enterprise.[18]

---

17. Sonfield (1976) found, however, that black business owners were much more disposed than their white counterparts toward a racially integrated clientele. If so, this puts the enclave hypothesis in the category of choice by default rather than preference as applied to minority entrepreneurship.

18. Data such as the *1982 Characteristics of Business Owners* (U.S. Bureau of the Census 1987) do not take into account differences in geographic location and concentration among minority groups. Although urbanization has developed rapidly among blacks, compared with

TABLE 4.8. SELF-EMPLOYMENT IN 1980 OF IMMIGRANTS ENTERING
THE UNITED STATES IN 1970–1980, BY COUNTRY OF ORIGIN
(in thousands)

Country of origin	Total employed	Self-employed	% self-employed
All countries	97,369	6,678	6.9
Foreign-born immigrants	2,541	104	4.1
Europe	368	21	5.7
Asia	771	43	5.6
Canada	52	4	7.7
Central America, Mexico	959	20	2.1
South America	145	5	3.4
Africa	59	3	5.1
Pre–1970 immigrants	991	316	31.9
Native-born	91,107	6,258	6.9

SOURCE: U.S. Bureau of the Census 1984b.

Immigration and Self-Employment

The low self-employment rates of minorities contrast sharply with those of
immigrants, who, currently as well as historically, have used self-
employment as a means of assimilation. Borjas (1986) has noted the relatively high and growing rates of self-employment among immigrants,
especially as compared to native-born workers in all racial categories. His
data, based on the 1980 census for men aged eighteen to sixty-four, show a
higher self-employment probability for the foreign-born than for the native-
born in each of six racial categories. Yuengert (1989) has confirmed this
finding for the same groups, comparing within each the self-employment
rates of the immigrant and native-born workers. Moreover, for each of three
immigrant cohorts and their native-born counterparts, self-employment
rates increased between 1970 and 1980.

Although interest in self-employment has been growing among recent immigrant cohorts, except for the relatively small and easily assimilable number of Canadians, their self-employment rates in 1980 generally were still
lower than those of all native-born employed workers (table 4.8).

Research among sociologists on immigrant self-employment has been
motivated by interest in the process of social and cultural assimilation. As-

---

Asian and Hispanic populations they have the highest levels of individuals living in nonurban
settings. Comparative application of the enclave hypothesis probably should take account of
this important difference.

similation is achieved when an immigrant or minority group achieves occupational status and income equivalent to or approaching the position of the native-born. Several sociologists have advanced as an underlying assumption the idea that the process of assimilation is a collective rather than an individual phenomenon, involving networks supported by intragroup solidarity and exchange (Light 1980; Cummings 1980; Fratoe 1986). This view is reflected in the so-called enclave hypothesis, outlined in the previous section, which asserts that self-employment and small business rates are higher the greater the degree of intragroup contact and solidarity.[19]

Although a few economists have taken up the question of the effect of enclaves on self-employment and relative earnings as an index of immigrant assimilation, sociologists have made the major contributions to this topic. Thus, in the recent sociological literature, we have Sanders and Nee's (1987) study of Cubans in Florida and Chinese in San Francisco; Evans's (1989) study of English- and non-English-speaking immigrants in Australia; Portes and Jensen's (1989) study of older and newer Cuban immigrants in Miami; and Zhou and Logan's (1989) study of New York City's Chinatown. Among economists, Borjas (1986) and Yuengert (1989) have dealt with the enclave effect on a national basis.

Intergroup differences in self-employment rates might, according to the enclave hypothesis, derive from intergroup differences in solidarity in an immigrant community. Thus Koreans in Los Angeles who have self-employment rates more than five times their population fraction (Light and Bonacich 1988) are implicitly more group-oriented than Greek immigrants, who tend to have relatively low rates of self-employment (Lovell-Troy 1980). In addition, cultural factors may augment the tendency to self-employment in certain ethnic communities. According to Light (1980), the small business in such communities caters to specialized cultural needs such as religious goods, group-specific foods and clothing, and personal services.

Among the above studies, there appears to be a consensus that membership in an enclave tends to increase the probability of self-employment. There is no consensus, however, on the effects of enclave membership on earnings and income. Sanders and Nee (1987), for example, have challenged the enclave hypothesis with respect to occupational and economic achievement in their comparative study of Cuban and Chinese immigrants.

---

19. The alternative hypothesis, of course, is that assimilation is basically a matter of individual preference, ability, and initiative, little different from the personal factors that presumably account for earnings differences among the native-born or already assimilated.

Statistically at least, members of these two ethnic groups, regardless of whether they were self-employed, did about as well outside a geographically defined enclave as inside. Portes and Jensen (1987), defending the enclave thesis, argue that Sanders and Nee confused place of work with place of residence. In terms of income differences, however, Sanders and Nee found evidence supporting the enclave hypothesis when *only* the self-employed in the two groups were considered. They concluded that, generally, there was no supporting basis for the enclave theory.

Borjas (1985 and 1986), moreover, concluded that self-employment in an enclave tended to lower earnings among the self-employed, mainly because of a quality or productivity difference between those immigrants employed inside the enclave and those employed outside, most of whom found jobs in the wage sector. Yuengert (1989) has reexamined Borjas's analysis, finding no significant difference between native-born and immigrant workers in the probability of self-employment but agreeing that self-employment in the enclave tended to depress earnings. Yuengert has added to the understanding of immigrant self-employment in finding a statistically significant and positive correlation between self-employment rates in the home country and the probability of self-employment in the United States.

The relationship between self-employment and immigration remains open for exploration, however. Borjas, for example, confesses that his finding on the enclave effect is an observation, not an explanation. Light and Bonacich (1988) indicate that the relationship is muddy. They raise the intriguing possibility that self-employment and small business growth may induce immigration by creating a favorable economic environment for the prospective immigrant, as in the case of the Koreans in Los Angeles. This hypothesis would be consistent with the finding of Borjas (1986) and Yuengert (1989) that the older the immigrant cohort, the greater the likelihood of self-employment.

All of the important empirical work on immigrant self-employment has been based on the experiences of men. The rates of self-employment may be relatively low among immigrant women because they are assisting their spouses in a family enterprise. It will be interesting to see if the general increase in self-employment among women has occurred among immigrant women as well.

Moonlighting and Part-Time Self-Employment

As suggested in chapter 2, the increase in self-employment could be attributed in part to a slower rate of overall economic growth. Holding multiple jobs, or "moonlighting," has always involved a relatively high rate of self-employment in the second job. Changes in the second-job self-employment rate might serve as a partial index of slower growth in the primary-job sectors. Data collected regularly by the Bureau of Labor Statistics show that the overall rate of multiple job-holding has remained fairly constant since the early 1960s (U.S. Department of Labor 1985). As a component of second jobs, however, self-employment has shown a marked increase since then, rising from one in five secondary jobs in the period 1962–66 to one in four in the early 1980s. The latter period, of course, was a period of recession during which unemployment rates rose to their highest level since the close of World War II. The shrinkage of opportunity in the wage and salary sector during that time may have led to the increase in self-employment among moonlighters.

The slowing economy of the late 1970s and early 1980s may also have accounted for the change in the level and nature of part-time employment among the self-employed. During the recession in the early 1980s, the pattern diverged from the general pattern. Though full-time jobs occupied about 95 percent of all workers in the periods 1970–74 and 1979–83, full-time employment in the latter period declined among the self-employed from 78 to 74 percent. Over the same period, 1979–83, involuntary part-time employment for economic reasons increased for all workers by 49 percent but by 121 percent for the self-employed (U.S. Department of Labor 1985). The apparent cyclical sensitivity of self-employment indicates a need to learn more about the characteristics that differentiate those who are marginally attached to self-employment from those who are more committed.

Professional Workers and the Incorporated Self-Employed

Though still relatively important, self-employment among the professions has been declining in importance since the close of World War II. The pattern has varied across professional groups, however, with the sharpest declines occurring in law and the health professions. Self-employment rates among the professional occupations serving business and industry have been stable or have increased moderately, especially among some of the newer professions. Some professional occupations such as teaching and engineering have never included large numbers of the self-employed. The postwar increase in incorporation, while not unique to self-employed professionals, is more common among nonprofessional occupations such as

TABLE 4.9. PERCENTAGE SELF-EMPLOYED IN SELECTED PROFES-
SIONAL OCCUPATIONS, BY GENDER, 1970 AND 1980

	Male		Female	
	1970	1980	1970	1980
All occupations	10.3	9.2	3.7	3.7
Professional and technical	10.7	12.4	4.0	4.3
Architects	31.5	30.0	20.0	20.7
Engineers	2.1	2.0	2.0	1.0
Computer specialists	0.4	1.9	0.2	1.5
Physicians	56.1	29.1	28.0	17.5
Dentists	86.7	62.4	33.3	25.0
Registered nurses	4.5	2.9	3.1	1.4
Lawyers and judges	54.2	42.4	30.8	14.9

SOURCES: U.S. Bureau of the Census 1973, 1984b.

construction, trade, and business and repair services. In 1983, incorporated self-employment accounted for about one-fourth of total self-employment (SBA, *State of Small Business, 1986*), and incomes were substantially greater than those of the unincorporated self-employed.

The basic pattern of self-employment across professional occupations has not undergone significant change in fifty to sixty years. In their study of five occupations in the 1930s, Friedman and Kuznets (1954) found the highest rates of independent practice in medicine, dentistry, and law. Engineers and certified public accountants had much lower rates. More than 80 percent of the two health professions were practicing in independent (usually solo) practices, and about 55 percent of the lawyers in the sample were also in independent practice, though some may have been in partnerships.

The postwar pattern is similar: self-employment rates are higher than the average of all professional and technical occupations in architecture, medicine, dentistry, and the law (table 4.9). The increase in the overall rate in the 1970–80 intercensal period has resulted primarily from an increase in some of the newer professional occupations, such as computing. Significantly, in the former strongholds of independent, usually solo, practice, there has been a steep decline in self-employment that cannot be accounted for by reclassification of the incorporated self-employed. In addition, invariably there are lower rates of self-employment among women in these professions. The increased number and proportion of professional women, because of this group's lower rates of self-employment, have been partly responsible for the overall decline in the health-diagnosing professions and law.

Although the trend for these groups has been downward since the pre–World War II period, the flight from self-employment appears to have accelerated during the 1970s. Sixty-one percent of physicians were in solo practice as late as 1966 (AMA 1984). By 1980, solo practice had declined to less than 50 percent (table 4.9). Until the beginning of the 1970s, the proportion of dentists in solo practice was holding at its long-term level of nearly 90 percent; by 1981, that fraction had declined to 66 percent, according to a survey of the American Dental Association (1982). The decline in solo practice occurred among both men and women, suggesting that more important factors than the increase in women practitioners were at work.

A preliminary review of the reasons for the decline of self-employment in the older professions reveals a set of complex demographic, economic, technological, and legal developments. Professional workers tend to become self-employed as they become older, having accrued the financial and human capital resources and sometimes the clientele necessary for entry and survival in their own practices. The increase in the size of entry-age cohorts in the health and legal professions in the last several decades has tended to reduce the average age of practitioners and thus may have depressed proportionately the probability of self-employment. According to American Medical Association data (1984), in 1983, 61 percent of physicians under thirty years of age were self-employed, while 80 percent of those older than thirty were so employed. To some degree, these age differences reflect cohort effects resulting from other factors including, for example, opportunities in other professions and occupations.

Technological developments, especially in the practice of medicine, have also tended to work against self-employment, in at least two ways. First, the development and introduction of advanced medical technologies and knowledge have increased the tendency toward specialization. Specialists are more likely than the general practitioner to practice in larger organizations because of the need for complementarity of skills and the capital cost of more expensive technologies. Even in dentistry, where general practice is still dominant, specialists are much less likely to be solo practitioners. In 1981, for example, 79 percent of general practitioners of dentistry were in solo practice, compared with 52 percent of specialists (American Dental Association 1982).

Economies of scale have also contributed to the decline in self-employment, notably, again, in the health-diagnosing professions. The sophisticated technologies needed to diagnose and treat health problems necessitate the purchase of expensive equipment and the employment of support and maintenance staff. From both a private and social viewpoint, solo practice becomes uneconomic; unit costs of service then have to be spread over a larger clientele than the average general practitioner sees.

Market size can also determine the type and scale of practice. Friedman and Kuznets (1954) included a market size variable in their study of five professions in the mid-1930s. Their data, though no longer current, show that for accountants, lawyers, and consulting engineers, there is a clear inverse relationship between community size and membership in a firm with other practitioners. In 1936, for example, 33 percent of the lawyers in the sample were members of multipractitioner firms in cities of 1.5 million or larger. In communities of 10,000 to 25,000, nonsolo practitioners accounted for only 23 percent of practicing attornies. No comparable data were provided on the relationship between the type of practice and community size for physicians and dentists. Although there are no supporting data, it is reasonable to expect lower rates of self-employment for these professions in larger communities, partly because specialists tend to locate in such communities and, as already noted, self-employment rates tend to be lower among specialists.

The decline of self-employment among lawyers is less understandable than that among health professionals. In the latter case, one suspects, specialization and economies of scale may be important underlying factors. By contrast, although there have been advances in the technology of law practice, especially the computerization of data and knowledge bases, it is difficult to believe that this development alone could have had a large role in changing the pattern of legal practice.

One possibly transient development that has led to the decline of solo practices among the professions as legal entities as defined by the IRS is the growth of the personal service corporation. As noted earlier, incorporated self-employment accounts for about one-quarter of total self-employment. Personal corporations were stimulated by the passage of state laws after the *Kintner* case in 1954. American Medical Association data indicate that by 1983, 54 percent of practicing physicians were incorporated, with the rate of incorporation particularly high among specialists. Personal incorporation has been less common in the professional occupations as a whole, however, than in the nonprofessional occupations, possibly because many professionals such as teachers and engineers are generally employed by conventional corporations.

Personal incorporation has been popular among some professions because of the tax advantages, including the ability to shelter retirement income contributions in Keogh-type pension plans and the exemption of business expenses from taxation. Incorporation may also have provided some protection against malpractice suits. The tax advantages have been considerably reduced by the Tax Equity and Fiscal Responsibility Act of 1982, which lowered the top tax rate. This development makes the further progress of personal incorporation uncertain, according to one discussion (Anspach and Snider 1984). Some advantages, however, such as protection against liability suits, may encourage some professionals to remain incorporated (Gould 1988).

There has been vigorous discussion of whether the decline of self-employment has endangered the essence of professionalism, namely, control over one's work. Derber (1982) and others have referred to the "proletarianization" of the professions. Others, notably Freidson (1986), have challenged this characterization. Many self-employed professionals, Freidson points out, are and always have been economically insecure and, consequently, dependent on the dictates of their clientele, rather than autonomous in the practice of their profession. Becoming a salaried member of an organization may mean a loss of economic independence but a gain in economic security. At the same time, Freidson believes that, as employees, professionals retain control over their work because of their ownership of specialized knowledge.

Self-employed professionals and the incorporated self-employed enjoy higher earnings on average than the nonprofessional, unincorporated self-employed. For example, median annual earnings of the incorporated self-employed in 1982 were more than twice those of the unincorporated self-employed (SBA, *State of Small Business, 1986*). For particular occupations, earnings data by class of worker are fragmentary. American Medical Association data for 1983 (American Medical Association 1984) show that physicians in nonsolo practice earned about 10 percent more than those in solo practice. In part, this figure reflects differences in the type of practice and degree of specialization. According to an earlier study, self-employed lawyers earn only about one-fifth the incomes of lawyers in firms with ten or more lawyers (Blaustein and Porter 1954). Friedman and Kuznets (1954) in their five-profession study found similar earnings relationships during the 1930s. Earnings ratios for multimember firms compared to solo practices ranged from 1.56 for certified public accountants to 2.14 for lawyers.

These findings are not surprising in light of earlier discussion about the decline of self-employment among the professions. In addition, one may speculate that in knowledge-based occupations incorporation may increase the degree of imperfection in the markets these occupations serve, especially in personal services such as medicine and law (Friedman and Kuznets 1954).

Self-Employed Employers

Since World War II, small businesses have been hailed as the principal job generators in the American economy. According to the SBA, for example, small businesses accounted for nearly two-thirds of the 10 million jobs created between 1980 and 1986 (SBA 1988). The same report indicates that small firms offer superior training and job experience, especially to first-time job seekers. Both claims are being challenged in a forthcoming study, reported on recently by Passell (1990), which indicates that small businesses destroy more jobs than large businesses, pay lower wages, and offer poorer on-the-job training.

The issue for this report is the extent to which self-employed workers become small business owners. Data are sparse, virtually nonexistent for the United States. In Britain, the self-employed accounted for 11 percent of total employment in 1984. Two-thirds of the self-employed had no employees, and only a little more than 2 percent employed more than twenty-five employees. Women were less likely to employ others; only 1 percent employed more than twenty-five persons (Creigh, Roberts, et al. 1986).[20] As far as I can discover, no studies have been made on the change from self-employed worker to employer. The data cited above indicate that in a majority of cases the self-employed are creating only their own jobs.

Poverty and Self-Employment

Given the lower earnings and incomes, on average, of the self-employed compared with wage and salary workers—ignoring occupational differences— it is not surprising to find an above-average incidence of poverty among the self-employed. Published data are not as current as would be desired; nonetheless, they indicate that the higher incidence of poverty among the self-employed appears to have become well established in the

---

20. These proportions did not change significantly in a later labor force survey in 1988 (Hakim 1989).

TABLE 4.10. NONFARM SELF-EMPLOYED AS PERCENTAGE OF LOW-INCOME EMPLOYED, AGES 22–64, BY GENDER, 1966–1972

Year	Male		Female	
	% self-employed	Self-employed as % low income	% self-employed	Self-employed as % low income
1966	8.1	–	4.6	–
1967	7.8	11.0	4.3	6.5
1968	8.0	13.8	4.4	5.8
1969	7.7	14.0	4.2	6.6
1970	7.8	16.4	4.2	7.1
1971	7.7	15.2	4.1	7.1
1972	7.7	15.7	4.2	6.1

SOURCE: U.S. Bureau of the Census 1974.

post–World War II period, with a noticeable upward trend in the early 1970s. Table 4.10 summarizes a comparison of the nonfarm self-employed as a percentage of total nonfarm employment with its share of the low-income working-age population.

Data based on householders rather than individuals suggest that the poverty level among the self-employed in recent years may have remained unchanged since 1972. For both sexes together, the proportion of self-employed householders in 1980 with incomes below the poverty level was nearly 22 percent, while the proportion of all self-employed householders was about 11 percent (U.S. Bureau of the Census 1981).

The Underground Economy

As discussed in the appendix, estimates of the numbers of self-employed may be affected to an unknown extent by the phenomenon variously known as the "black," "irregular," or "underground" economy. In principle, self-employment provides an excellent opportunity for off-the-books work, to use the British expression. Evasion of taxes, avoidance of regulation, and engagement in illicit activities are alleged to be the major reasons for unrecorded employment. Such activities leave few traces, of course, so that efforts to identify the employment practices involved are largely frustrated. That nonreporting and underreporting of taxable earnings and income are disproportionately high among the self-employed is not, however, in dispute.

A U.S. General Accounting Office study (1981) that compared income tax and Social Security tax reports with those persons reporting as self-employed in the CPS found that 16 percent of the self-employed did not report taxable income either to the IRS or the Social Security Administration. The self-employed may account for as much as one-quarter of unreported income, according to an IRS study cited by Carson (1984) in her review of efforts to measure the underground economy. Much of the unreported income is believed to be derived from illicit activities, possibly as much as half according to one estimate (Simon and Witte 1982). Among the visible self-employed, however, it is more common for personal income to be underreported or concealed in exempt business expenses. For that group at least, the various studies suggest that the count of the self-employed is only marginally affected by the underground economy but that the measurement of income and earnings may be more seriously understated.

Conclusion

In this chapter the various social and demographic groups that compose the self-employed have been reviewed to determine factors that may account for their differences from wage and salary workers. The probability of self-employment and the relative earnings of each subgroup was examined. A major portion of the chapter was devoted to women as an increasingly significant component of nonfarm self-employment both in the United States and other countries. Self-employment among racial and ethnic minorities and recent immigrants was also discussed. Finally, notice was taken of other interesting subgroups, including the incorporated, professionals, the impoverished, and self-employed employers.

With respect to the two major groups—women and racial and ethnic minorities—the data and analyses thus far indicate a degree of consensus on the probability of self-employment. For both groups, self-employment appears to be a process of self-selection, driven in the two cases in different directions and by different factors. Self-employed women differ little from their wage and salary counterparts in their observable social and cultural characteristics, human capital endowments, and market opportunities. As a tentative hypothesis, consequently, one is led to conclude that women who enter self-employment, in addition to having such broad motivations as increased autonomy and higher incomes, have work and leisure preference patterns that distinguish them from women in wage jobs. The factors that underly this difference will probably be found in the contexts of family and household employment decisions, such as those based on marital status, number of earners in the household, and differences in the degree and nature of dependency. A few of the studies examined have taken some account of these contexts, but much more work needs to be done.

Understanding the marked earnings disadvantage of self-employed women depends in part on the particular comparison one is making. The lower earnings of self-employed women relative to self-employed men are attributable mainly to gender differences in industrial and occupational distributions and to the smaller scale and relatively lower levels of capitalization of women's enterprises. Although the process of socialization and institutional factors may bear some responsibility for such differences, the relatively more favorable earnings positions of self-employed women in other countries casts strong doubt on the universality of this explanation.

We have no satisfactory explanation for the earnings differences between employed and self-employed women. Since this difference has not been subject to analysis, one can only fall back on the hypothesis that there are differences in attitudes toward work and career, located again, most probably, in the contexts of family and household. The trade-offs in earnings that self-employed women may make deserve intensive investigation.

Racial and ethnic minorities, including blacks, have increased their various rates of self-employment during the past decades. Yet, relative to their populations, in comparison with nonminority males, most of these groups are underrepresented in self-employment. The underrepresentation of black workers is particularly marked and not easy to explain. In theory, self-employment should provide a shield against discrimination and the possibility of choosing a more supportive market, especially in large urban areas. The evidence so far, however, suggests that this may not be the case. Blacks with better human capital choose wage employment and higher earnings over self-employment. The enclave hypothesis may not be valid for blacks, it has been suggested, because they are not sufficiently isolated from the labor market and thus are exposed to the competition of the nonminority self-employed.

The influence of the enclave on self-employment among recent immigrant populations is unclear. The studies reviewed tend to agree that, depending on how the enclave is defined, membership can increase the probability of self-employment. But whether self-employment in an enclave serves to increase or decrease relative earnings is moot. Macro-oriented studies, mainly by economists, tend to the negative influence, while micro-oriented studies mostly conclude otherwise or find no effect.

The decline of self-employment among the personal service professions, resulting from complex economic, technological, and institutional factors, has nevertheless left those occupations with above-average self-employment rates and with above-average earnings for salaried professionals. The decline has been driven in part by the withdrawal of tax advantages and, in larger part, by technological and organizational factors. More data and analysis of these developments are needed.

The higher incidence of poverty among the self-employed is related to their employment and earnings opportunities. As more is learned about those aspects of self-employment, more will be understood about its relationship to poverty. Whether the increasing rate of self-employment is also generating overall increases in nonfarm employment, as self-employment is transformed into small business ownership, is an open question. Whether both can be true simultaneously—whether there can be a high and possibly increasing growth in poverty among the self-employed at the same time as self-employment is the leading sector of job growth—is worthy of resolution.

In very broad terms, I have uncovered the complexity of self-employment as a social and cultural phenomenon. Though there have been important changes in the position of the various groups engaged in self-employment, its basic structure has remained largely intact in the post–World War II period. Self-employment has responded to some of the broad social and economic changes during this period, notably the increasing rate and commitment of women to the labor market and the continuing shift in job opportunities from the goods to the service sector. But in some respects it has also been resistant to such changes, probably in part because of intrinsic structural limitations on opportunities for self-employment and because the mechanisms for institutional change among the self-employed are undeveloped, perhaps inherently.

CHAPTER FIVE

Government and Self-Employment

Since the 1920s at least, the government has been an increasingly important presence in the mainstream labor market of employers and employees. Public policy has shaped the employer-employee relationship in a variety of ways. Through laws and public programs, it has sought to reduce the incidence and severity of unemployment and industrial accidents and disease. It has provided health insurance and income protection for older Americans and helped develop a well-trained labor force. Government policy has also sought to eliminate discrimination and increase economic opportunity for persons who have been at a disadvantage because of race, gender, or disability.

Self-employment invokes an image of freedom or, alternatively, exclusion from government intervention. Except for the contractual legal obligations of Anglo-American common law and the payment of taxes associated with the provision of goods and services, the self-employed individual is believed to enjoy the free pursuit of self-interest inherent in the doctrine of laissez-faire. This conception is incomplete and misleading. It probably derives from a tendency to regard self-employment as a form of business enterprise, rather than recognizing its kinship to paid employment.

In reality, there is a threefold relationship between government and self-employment. First, governments in the United States and other countries have developed programs intended to encourage the growth of self-employment. In some instances, there has been direct support and subsidy of the self-employed, including preference in government purchasing of goods and services. In other cases, growth has been encouraged by exemption from or mitigation of regulations imposed on business enterprises generally. Second, the government regulates self-employment to protect public health and safety. In this case, occupational and business licensing are the principal vehicles of public policy. In the first two areas, the government influences self-employment indirectly. In the third area, the social protection of the self-employed as workers, government treats self-employment directly and explicitly as a labor problem deserving of public policy.

In the United States, the development of programs for the self-employed and the social protection of the self-employed as workers are primarily federal responsibilities. Although there is some federal involvement in the protection of public health and safety, this is principally the responsibility of state and local governments. In this chapter, the three dimensions of the relationship of government to self-employment are discussed in broad terms. For comparison, developments in other countries are also presented. Documentation and interpretation of the policies and programs discussed in this chapter are often ambiguous since most of these policies and programs are directed either to business firms or to specific occupations, making generalizations difficult. Self-employment may take any of the legal forms of business organization, further complicating the effort to obtain a clear picture of the various relationships between government and the strictly self-employed. Nonetheless, the description of self-employment as a labor market phenomenon would be incomplete without attention to these institutional features. Before beginning the survey, however, it is useful to identify self-employment as a significant component of small business, since much of the literature does not make this explicit.

The Small Business Administration identifies small businesses as those firms or establishments employing fewer than five hundred employees. In those industries in which self-employment is most prominent, average firm size is generally very small. Calculations made by the author from the 1982 economic censuses show that 75 percent of the small businesses in retail trade employed fewer than ten employees and 31 percent employed none at all. In the service industries, 80 percent of small firms employed fewer than ten workers. In construction, 67 percent had no payroll; among individual proprietors, who comprise 71 percent of all construction firms, 88 percent were strictly self-employed. In 1982, these three industries alone accounted for more than 90 percent of all establishments employing fewer than five hundred employees. Thus it is a fair inference that self-employment is a dominant feature of the small business economy and that government policies directed specifically toward small businesses will have significant effects on the self-employed.

Government Support

Government support of self-employment appears to be motivated by both ideological and economic concerns. Since self-employment epitomizes self-reliance and independence, government support of self-employment and small businesses encourages the idea of a democratic society, rather than one in which political and economic power is concentrated in large business corporations, trade unions, and government itself. Furthermore, small businesses and, by implication, self-employment are seen as the locus of economic dynamism—a principal source of technological creativity and innovation and the major generator of new jobs (Birch and MacCracken 1985)—and as a bulwark against monopolistic tendencies in the economy. Because the economies of scale available to large businesses are less available to small businesses and individual entrepreneurs (Berney and Owens 1985), it is believed that without government support the social and economic advantages of a strong small business sector would be lost.

In broad terms, the government has supported self-employment in two ways: directly, through the provision of financial and technical assistance, and indirectly, through the removal or exemption of small businesses from regulation. The government may also indirectly create a more favorable climate for small business by, for example, vigorously enforcing antitrust legislation and protecting the demand for the services of self-employed entrepreneurs through business and occupational licensing. Public programs that reduce some of the economic risk of entrepreneurship, such as coverage under the Social Security law, may also encourage the growth of self-employment.

There is no clear line distinguishing the roles and responsibilities of the local, state, and federal government in promoting small business and supporting self-employment. The federal government has provided loans and preferential procurement to small businesses. Some state and local governments also maintain industrial and economic development programs that provide start-up opportunities for entrepreneurs, and most regulatory relief and licensing is at state and local government levels. Social protection of the self-employed, both in the United States and abroad, however, is primarily the responsibility of the central government.

FINANCIAL SUPPORT PROGRAMS

Businesses of all sizes must have access to finance if they are to become established or expand. Established businesses and new ventures of average size can usually obtain finance from commercial banks and other institutional lenders, including the equity and bond markets. Such sources are rarely available to the very small business, especially in its start-up period. Analysis of the differences in the financing of large and small businesses suggests that the monitoring and information costs to the lender, relative to the size of the loan, often make financing of small enterprises unprofitable (SBA, *State of Small Business, 1987*). Consequently, such enterprises more often must rely initially on so-called angel money, that is, personal savings and loans from friends and relatives or other informal sources of venture capital. Suppliers other than employees may also extend credit on a short-term basis. Inadequate financing often contributes to the failure of small businesses and hinders the entry of certain groups into small business.

Since World War II, the federal government has supplemented the personal and informal sources of financing for small businesses. Its principal vehicle is the Small Business Administration, which was established in 1953 in part as a reaction to the alleged bias toward big business of the Reconstruction Finance Corporation, which up to that time was the federal government's major provider of business loans (Chase 1973). The lending programs of the SBA, it was hoped, would supplement the effort to improve the competitive environment, mainly through enforcement of antitrust regulations.

The SBA provides small business loans to applicants and loan guarantees to private lenders. The principal direct lending vehicles of the SBA are the Small Business Investment Companies and the Minority Business Investment Companies. From 1980 to 1987, the number of firms receiving disbursements under these two programs increased from 2,637 to 4,128. Total disbursements doubled during the period, reaching about $680 million in 1987. Lending to minority businesses tripled during the period, increasing from 21 to 39 percent of assisted firms (SBA, *State of Small Business, 1989*). The SBA also guarantees loans to qualified small business applicants. In 1984, loan guarantees in dollar terms were approximately twice the level of direct borrowing under the federal programs.

State and local governments also provide financial support, information, and training services for new business ventures. Frequently, such programs are designed to enhance the economic development of the state or locality.

GOVERNMENT PURCHASING

The other principal method of direct support of small business is through government purchases of goods and services. As in the case of loans and

TABLE 5.1. DISTRIBUTION OF FEDERAL PRIME CONTRACTS, BY PRODUCT OR SERVICE CATEGORY AND BUSINESS SIZE, FISCAL YEARS 1979 AND 1987 (in thousands of dollars)

Product/service	1979		1987	
	All awards	Small business share	All awards	Small business share
Total	$88,211,626	15.8%	$197,275,512	17.9%
Research and development	12,789,324	6.6	27,001,387	6.9
Construction	7,544,603	47.8	13,069,520	50.7
Other services	23,314,124	13.2	44,332,169	14.3
Supplies and equipment	44,615,175	14.5	89,111,778	12.5

SOURCE: SBA, *State of Small Business, 1989.*

loan guarantees, the federal government leads in this area of assistance to small business. Beginning in 1942, through various legislation, the federal government has directed its agencies to allocate a share of its purchases to small businesses. The most recent development was the passage in 1982 of the Small Business Innovation Development Act, which is intended to help small businesses obtain a larger share of federally funded research and development grants through agency set-asides.

The impact on small businesses of the federal procurement program has been sizable, especially with respect to small awards and contracts. In fiscal 1987, small businesses received about $35 billion in prime contracts and an estimated $26 billion in subcontracts. The sum of these awards accounted for 31 percent of total federal procurement (SBA, *State of Small Business, 1989*). Small firms received about 46 percent of the smaller awards (until recently, under $10,000, now under $25,000) in that year but only about 15 percent of the larger awards. Prime contract awards to small businesses have remained constant at about 15 percent of the total since 1979. Small businesses have been relatively more successful in obtaining contracts in construction but less successful in other areas (table 5.1).

The practice of preferential procurement has been criticized on economic grounds. In a recent study of procurement awards by the Department of Housing and Urban Development (HUD), Hebert and Becker (1985) concluded that small businesses are at no technical disadvantage in competing for government contracts. In fact, according to the study, the bids made by small businesses were generally lower than the bids submitted by large firms. The study was based on contract proposals for awards greater than $10,000, however, and therefore is probably not representative of small business contractors as a whole.

Federal government procurement is also used to encourage small business ownership among women and socially and economically disadvantaged minorities. Data reported by the SBA in its annual report for 1989 show that in fiscal 1987, businesses owned by women or minorities increased their shares of prime contract awards over the previous year, despite an overall decline in the share of prime contracts to small businesses. The relative shares of these two groups have not advanced significantly in recent years, though new legislation and administrative directives are expected to improve the benefit to the federal government of purchasing goods and services from businesses owned by women or minorities. According to several studies, however, federal programs have had little effect on the growth of minority-owned small businesses (Garvin 1973; Ando 1986).

STATE GOVERNMENT PURCHASING

State governments also use their purchasing power to support small businesses. In most states, the dollar terms used in the legal definition of a small business are lower than those used by the federal government. A special report estimates that in 1984–85 state governments purchased about $25 billion worth of goods and services from small businesses, possibly representing about 27 percent of purchases or, in relative terms, nearly twice the level of federal small business procurement (SBA, *State of Small Business, 1987*).

ASSISTANCE TO THE UNEMPLOYED AND POOR

A number of countries have experimented with, and at least two have established, programs intended to encourage unemployed and low-income workers to become self-employed. Pilot experiments are just beginning in the United States. The assumption is that given financial and other support, some members of these groups will be motivated to create their own jobs and perhaps to generate jobs for others. There is no expectation that such programs will of themselves resolve the problems of unemployment and poverty.[1] In these experimental programs, unemployment insurance benefits are paid to workers who start their own businesses and thus become self-employed. In most countries, including the United States, self-employment would normally disqualify workers for unemployment benefits.

France established its program in 1979, and Britain did in 1982.[2] Eight other countries also permit payment of unemployment insurance and other forms of public assistance to unemployed individuals who turn to self-employment.[3] The British Enterprise Allowance Scheme provides unemployment insurance benefits for up to one year, provided eligible participants produce at least £1,000 as start-up capital. This program became permanent in 1986, and it was expected that there would be 100,000 new participants in 1987–88 ("Two Years after the Enterprise Allowance Scheme" 1986).

An early Department of Employment study of the British program found an overall survival rate of 86 percent in the first fifteen months after start-up; 61 percent of those who were in the program for the full year were still self-employed two years after termination of the allowance. Approximately two-thirds of these enterprises have been in personal and business services. The balance was divided between construction and retail trade (Allen and Hunn 1985). An evaluation conducted three years after the establishment of the program surveyed participants who were in the same business two years after termination of their allowance. A multivariate analysis found that the most important factors affecting survival were age, a spouse working part time, and the amount of capital the participant intended to invest in the first year ("Two Years after the Enterprise Allowance Scheme" 1986). More than 90 percent of the program participants were men.

The French Unemployed Entrepreneurs program provides a lump-sum payment that varies with the length of unemployment and the speed with which the business is established. In addition to the subsidy in lieu of unemployment insurance benefits, beneficiaries receive the same social security coverages as wage and salary workers. Bendinck and Egan's (1987)

---

1. Balkin (1989) has developed a model to estimate the number of net new jobs that would be created by a supported self-employment program. Under varying assumptions and based on 1984 data on the low-income population, his estimates of new jobs range from 400,000 to 7 million. The latter number, it may be pointed out, exceeds the average number of unemployed in the United States in that year. The model is not specific, however, about the period of time required to reach any of the job creation targets.

2. For a description of the programs in these two countries, see Bendinck and Egan (1987) and Balkin (1989).

3. Among them are Australia and New Zealand, according to Creigh, Roberts, et al. (1986).

study of these two programs concludes that supported self-employment is not a panacea for the hard-core unemployed and may be too costly even for those programs in which participants are more likely to succeed. Both the Department of Employment and Bendick and Egan report higher survival rates for those with greater financial and human capital resources, who were more likely to enter self-employment even without government subsidy. The macroeconomic effects of these programs have not yet received appropriate attention. A major concern in such a study will be whether supported self-employment is a zero-sum game, that is, whether self-employment displaces employed workers through product or labor market competition.

Under the sponsorship of the U.S. Department of Labor, an experiment and pilot study program similar to the French program has been started in Washington State. As described by Kilborn (1990), one thousand individuals will be chosen from among unemployment insurance applicants who apply. Half the group, chosen by random selection, will receive unemployment benefits in a lump sum; the other half will receive benefits in the normal monthly fashion. Both groups will be required to take business training; lump-sum recipients, in addition, will be required to prepare an acceptable business plan. Benefits paid during the period of preparation of the plan will be deducted from the individual's total allowable benefit, thus reducing the size of the lump sum.[4] According to the initial report, fewer than 5 percent of the unemployed had applied for the program.

Prior to the establishment of the Washington experiment, a few states, namely, California, Oregon, and Michigan, largely on an ad hoc basis, have permitted benefits to individuals who enter self-employment during a period of benefit eligibility. In Michigan, benefits continue only as long as the beneficiary continues an active search for wage employment (Commerce Clearing House), which is probably the general rule in such cases.

A number of states are currently experimenting with self-employment programs as a means by which people can leave the welfare rolls and break the poverty cycle. Balkin (1989) advocates such assistance, at least as a stopgap, and suggests augmenting the human capital as well as the incomes

---

4. The intent of this provision is not clear but may be designed to discourage malingering and abuse. It will be interesting to observe how it affects the incentive to become self-employed and the probability of survival of the business. On its face, it would seem to produce less adequate business plans and reduce the start-up capital needed to increase the likelihood of survival.

of low-income and disadvantaged persons. He believes self-employment helps prepare those who lack work experience for more rewarding opportunities in wage employment.

A recent account by Hinds (1990) notes that experimental programs are already established or are being mounted in a number of states, usually on a one-year basis.[5] Volunteer participants in these programs receive business training, career counseling, and, in some states, start-up loans if they do not have sufficient assets from other sources. In all of these programs, federal and state rules on welfare eligibility are waived so that participants may, for example, use savings to start their own businesses.

Although there are anecdotal reports of individual successes, the overall success of self-employment as a way to escape poverty is yet to be known. Recent studies of poverty and self-employment are not optimistic. Bauman (1988), for example, studied the characteristics of the low-income self-employed in a five-state area. Using a 1980 census sample of full-time workers, he found that the self-employment rate among the low-income workers was twice that of all workers in the sample. The low-income self-employed were distributed across industries in much the same way as all self-employed, and the distributions of demographic characteristics among the two groups were similar. Mangum and Tansky (1988) studied an experimental program that offered self-employment training and support for the economically disadvantaged. They were skeptical whether this approach offered a significant escape from poverty. Self-employment for some individuals may be symptomatic of low incomes and poverty, as suggested in chapter 3, rather than a relief from it.

Indirect and Nonfinancial Support

Several indirect and, in some cases, nonfinancial government measures may encourage entry into and growth of self-employment. These measures include relief from business taxation, regulation, and antitrust enforcement. Similar measures, which are more problematic but which have some potential for stimulating self-employment, are occupational licensing and policies that provide social protection and income security for the self-employed. The supportive effects of these measures have received little in the way of evaluation, so it is difficult to do more than simply call attention to them.

---

5. The states are New Jersey, Maryland, Michigan, Mississippi, North Carolina, Pennsylvania, and West Virginia.

Tax evasion, as noted earlier, may be an important motivation for entering into self-employment and small business ownership. If it is true that relatively high marginal income tax rates induce entry into self-employment,[6] then their reduction should discourage such entrepreneurship. If it is desirable to encourage self-employment and small business, other tax measures can be considered. Exemption from or a lower rate of business and sales taxes is one approach; another is to offer tax credits for job creation, one of the outcomes expected from encouraging small business growth.

Deregulation

Relief from regulations and the associated burden of paperwork has been the major means of indirect support of small business in the United States. The deregulation movement of the 1970s and 1980s, which affected mainly transportation and financial services, has largely superseded classical antitrust law as a means of maintaining competitive markets. The underlying rationale is that the small enterprise is at a competitive disadvantage in complying with regulations and preparing proposals for government contracts. Because it does not enjoy the economies of scale of larger businesses, the costs of compliance and of contract preparation and administration act like a regressive tax on the small business (Berney and Owens 1985; Aram and Coomes 1985; Brock, Evans, and Phillips 1986). Cole and Tegeler (1980) list the costs as including licenses, record keeping, fines for noncompliance, and the diversion of management from its principal duties. They estimate that in 1980, on average, businesses of all sizes were subject to regulation by a combination of seven federal, state, and local agencies. In the case of industries typically populated by small businesses, state and local agencies predominate.

A variety of regulatory relief measures have already been passed in response to the situation outlined above. Under the federal Occupational Safety and Health Act, for example, firms employing fewer than ten employees are exempt from routine inspection. On a broader scale, the Regulatory Flexibility Act and the Paperwork Reduction Act, both passed in 1980, provide for simplification, consolidation, and reduction in the number of forms required under various federal programs. Although these acts are not specific to firm size, small enterprises will benefit the most.

---

6. But see chapter 2, where the evidence in support of a tax effect is by no means clear.

As noted earlier, however, the issue of scale diseconomies as the rationale for regulatory relief has not gone unchallenged. There is the HUD study referred to above (Hebert and Becker 1985). In addition, a study of pollution abatement and firm size by Brock, Evans, and Phillips (1986) found that while the capital costs of abatement discouraged the entry of small establishments during 1967–77, small single-unit established businesses enjoyed a distinct advantage over large and/or multiunit firms in per-employee cost.

In its review of the effects of deregulation in the transportation and financial services industries, the SBA (*State of Small Business, 1987*) concluded that their share of employment growth between 1980 and 1984 exceeded their share of employment at the beginning of the period by 38 percent. In nonwater transportation, firms employing fewer than one hundred employees accounted for the entire net gain in employment. In financial services, firms of this size accounted for more than one-third of the sector's job growth. These industries are not the locus of most of the growth in self-employment,[7] however; it is probable that most of the growth industries are located in the corporate sector.

Regulation of Self-Employment

Most laws regulating self-employment are state and local. This is reinforced by federal regulatory relief and by the fact that most self-employment does not include interstate commerce. The bulk of the legislation is geared toward public health and safety. Because so much of it is specific to particular industries or occupations, however, it is difficult to generalize about its effects on employment and earnings in self-employment. The complexity of this body of regulation as it affects self-employment can be somewhat reduced by dividing the field into two parts. One part deals with business enterprises per se and is not usually specific to the self-employed. The other is person-specific and often, as in the case of occupational licensing, intended to safeguard public health and safety. Further measures, primarily in the area of social protection, address self-employment as an issue of labor utilization rather than regulation.

---

7. In transportation, for example, railroads, airlines, interurban passenger and freight motor transportation. In financial services, the likelihood of self-employment is somewhat greater, for example, in insurance and real estate.

GENERAL REGULATION

Taxation has the broadest reach of any regulation, affecting all enterprises regardless of size or legal form of business organization. At the state and local levels, but not in all jurisdictions, income, sales, and property taxes reach all private enterprises. In some industries, small firms operating on thin margins may be at a competitive disadvantage because of taxes. Consequently, there is constant pressure for tax exemption in industries that are domains of self-employment. Foods consumed at home and personal clothing, for example, are frequently exempt from sales taxes. New York State exempts from sales tax materials used in the construction, renovation, or repair of residences and businesses, which affect small, often self-employed contractors. Recently, New York also exempted equipment, tools, and materials used in the production of goods with a useful life of less than one year and the installation and maintenance of such tools and equipment (New York State Department of Commerce, Division for Small Business n.d.).

A more direct impact on self-employment results from business licensing. Almost every field of business is subject to some licensure. In addition to paying a fee for the license, the entrepreneur may be required to meet technical or financial qualifications and may also be subject to inspection and audit with the risk of license suspension or revocation. In addition to occupational licensing discussed below, a large number and variety of enterprises in which self-employment is common are subject to licensure. In New York, the state government requires nearly 1,200 licenses (New York State, Office of Business Permits 1987), which regulate such businesses as restaurants, cafes, and clubs serving alcoholic beverages; the producers of alcoholic beverages; dairies; insurance agents; undertakers; taxidermists; pawnbrokers; real estate brokers; midwives; and well drillers.

Licensing is even more extensive at the local government level. In New York State, again, towns, villages, cities, and counties all have constitutional authority to license and regulate such enterprises as taxis and buses, circuses, theaters, bowling alleys, restaurants, and food retailers. The degree to which this authority is utilized and its effect on the growth or survival of small businesses is unknown.

OCCUPATIONAL LICENSING

Self-employment is probably more directly affected by the licensing or certification of occupations than of businesses. Shimberg (1985) estimates that as many as eight hundred different occupations and trades may be licensed in the United States, but this may be an undercount considering that the extent of occupational licensing at the local government level is largely unknown. In an earlier study, Shimberg, Esser, and Kruger (1972) refer to Dade County, Florida, where eighty different kinds of construction contractors are required to carry distinctive licenses. The same study speaks of the growth of local licensing as "haphazard" and "chaotic." In New York, the state licenses seventy-five different occupations. The majority of the occupations licensed by state and local governments commonly include self-employed workers. Exceptions are airplane pilots, maritime deck officers, and securities salespersons, all of whom are subject to federal licensing.

An occupational license is a grant of authority to practice an occupation given to those individuals who have met relevant standards of training and demonstrated competence. The official rationale for such grants is the protection of public health and safety. In most jurisdictions, unlicensed practice is unlawful in the case of the so-called independent professions and some other occupations. The intervention of the licensing body in market processes is often justified on one or more of the following grounds: the existence of market imperfection; externalities, especially the potential for harm or exploitation by an unlicensed practitioner; or information asymmetry between the provider and the purchaser of the goods and services (Horowitz 1980). A license, in brief, is a grant of monopoly in which it is assumed that the public benefit outweighs the cost of noncompetition.

For certain professional occupations, such as law, medicine, architecture, and accounting, the monopoly is granted to the profession rather than to individual practitioners.[8] In exchange, such professions are self-regulating, not only in assuring the competency of their members but in curbing noncompetitive tendencies. In the United States, these professions enjoy de facto immunity from antitrust legislation. Similar policies are observed abroad. In Australia in 1974, for example, law, medicine, dentistry, and accounting were given explicit legal immunity from antitrust actions. Since then, other professions have asked for similar protection (Nieuwenhuysen and Williams-Wynn 1982).

The protection from competition that is afforded by licensing may be one of the factors sustaining the relatively high rates of self-employment among

---

8. Of course, individual practitioners may also benefit directly from possession of an exclusive license, depending on the market for their services and the availability of substitutes.

TABLE 5.2. PERCENTAGE SELF-EMPLOYED AMONG SELECTED PROFES-
SIONAL AND TECHNICAL OCCUPATIONS, BY GENDER, 1970 AND 1980

	1970		1980	
	Male	Female	Male	Female
Architects	30.8	23.8	30.0	20.7
Accountants	11.7	5.5	12.0	3.2
Chiropractors	92.7	90.0	N.A.	N.A.
Dental hygienists	66.7	1.2	N.A.	N.A.
Lawyers[a]	56.8	34.4	25.3	10.3
Licensed practical nurses	5.7	3.9	2.5	1.8
Optometrists	78.5	57.1	N.A.	N.A.
Pharmacists	23.2	12.2	10.0	2.3
Podiatrists	88.9	50.0	N.A.	N.A.
Physicians	56.2	28.2	20.2	12.2
Registered nurses	6.4	3.4	2.2	1.2
Surveyors	4.9	5.5	14.3	4.9
Veterinarians	60.5	30.0	N.A.	N.A.

SOURCES: U.S. Bureau of the Census 1973, 1984b.
[a]Includes judges.

the professions.[9] Despite a decline in those rates in recent years, self-employment rates in law and the health professions remain relatively high among both men and women (table 5.2). Informational asymmetry is prevalent among these occupations, since their services tend to be client-specific and increasingly specialized (Evans 1980; Weingast 1980; Young 1985).

According to the theory of self-regulation, the market power of the practitioner in such transactions needs to be restrained by a moral obligation (e.g., a code of ethics) and the quasi-legal authority of a professional association (Berlant 1975; Cullen 1978). There is a consensus that licensing of the professions, usually effected by a practitioner-dominated board, serves, in Freidson's (1986) term, a "gate-keeping" function (see also Gilb 1966; Gellhorn 1976; Ostry 1978; Young 1985).

The principal issues associated with self-employment and occupational licensing concern entry into the occupation and the effect of entry on earnings. There is practically no literature in this area. Most of the labor eco-

---

9. There may be a number of small business associations similar to professional associations which among other objectives attempt to control entry. They probably are found at the local or state level.

nomics literature has been concerned with the effect of licensing on interstate mobility of the independent professions and has ignored differences in employment settings. Beginning with Holen (1965), whose findings have largely been confirmed by others (Pashigian 1979, 1980; Boulier 1980), studies have found significant interoccupational differences in geographic mobility and in the dispersion of earnings attributable to mandatory licensing. None of the studies, however, distinguishes the self-employed solo practitioner from other forms of business organization.

Rayack (1975) and Freeman (1980) have studied the effect of licensure in selected nonprofessional occupations. Using data for three New England states and twelve licensed occupations, Rayack tested the relationship between examination failure rates and industry unemployment rates. Statistically significant positive correlations were found for ten of the twelve occupations. Freeman studied the history of the representation of blacks in licensed skilled crafts. From 1880 to 1890, blacks were underrepresented in licensed occupations compared with their representation in unlicensed trades of comparable skill levels. From 1960 to 1970, by contrast, though Freeman found black workers to be underrepresented in proportion to their numbers in the working-age population, there was no difference in their representation in licensed and unlicensed skilled occupations.

As noted, few of the foregoing studies differentiate between the self-employed and other classes of workers. Freeman (1980), in testing the effect of licensing on the entry of black workers, reports that in both decades self-employment as an independent variable had a negative effect on the representation of blacks. This is consistent with the conclusions of the earlier discussion of the underrepresentation of blacks in self-employment. The effect of licensure on earnings in self-employment is unknown. In principle, other things being equal, there should be no effect, since all practitioners regardless of type of employment are legally required to be licensed. One can hypothesize, however, that unlicensed practitioners, if they could be distinguished, would offer their services at a lower price than licensed practitioners.

Social Protection

Social protection is the one area in which governments have recognized that the self-employed are subject to the same hazards as wage and salary workers. Failure of one's own business may mean a spell of unemployment as well as the loss of physical and financial capital. Illness and disability interrupt or reduce the flow of income for the self-employed entrepreneur just as they do for the wage and salary worker, unless there is provision for income loss under employee benefit and welfare programs. The self-employed worker has more control over the timing of retirement; at some point, however, he or she also must consider the need to maintain income when work stops. The increase in nonfarm self-employment and the changes in its demographic and social structure in many industrialized countries has led the International Labor Organization (International Labour Office 1990) to call for a reexamination and reevaluation of social welfare policies "originally conceived for employees in full-time regular employment."

Coverage of self-employment under the principal social welfare programs involves important policy decisions that are usually less of an issue in the coverage of employees. These decisions concern "moral hazard" in that the self-employed worker has a greater degree of control over the incidence and perhaps also the urgency of the need for income protection. For example, is the unemployment of a self-employed worker a "no-fault" development beyond the individual's control? Should the self-employed worker be eligible for workers' compensation if he or she has control over the working environment, how tools and equipment are maintained and used, and so on? By providing protection against such market risks, governments implicitly acknowledge the similarity of employed and self-employed workers. In the case of the latter, however, the costs of protection are borne by or charged to self-employed individuals and the safeguards against abuse take account of the greater degree of discretion and control among the self-employed.

Self-employed workers in the United States are covered under the Social Security Act for retirement income, including retirement because of disability, and in some states, such as New York, they enjoy a tax subsidy of private pensions comparable to that afforded wage and salary workers. Insurance under public programs against income loss due to illness, injury, or disease, work-connected or not, is virtually nonexistent. Unemployment insurance for previously self-employed persons is also not available, though, as noted earlier, in some states self-employment does not automatically disqualify an individual from receiving benefits. In general, in most other industrialized countries, as in the United States, protection of the self-employed is less comprehensive and/or more restrictive than the protection provided wage and salary workers.

Retirement income programs are by far the most comprehensive of the social protection programs in all countries that cover self-employed workers under protective labor legislation. A survey completed in 1973 of twenty-seven countries reported that only four—Cuba, the U.S.S.R., Iran, and New Zealand—did not include self-employed workers in public old-age benefit schemes. The first two countries, at that time at least, did not accord official status to the self-employed (David 1973). The same study reported that in twenty-three countries, occupationally specific pension programs also included the self-employed. In all these programs, self-employed and wage and salary workers were treated alike with respect to types of benefits, including retirement, disability, and survivors' benefits.

Mandatory coverage of both farm and nonfarm self-employed workers under the old-age benefit program of the Social Security Act is now virtually complete in the United States. The principal outstanding issue, which is expected to be resolved in the near future, is the equalization of the total self-employed tax rate with the combined employer-employee tax rate. Mandatory coverage began with the nonfarm self-employed in 1951 and became universal with the inclusion of the learned professions in 1957. The benefit pattern is similar to that of other industrialized countries, and no distinction is made between self-employed and wage and salary workers. Part-time self-employed workers are covered by the benefit program, provided they are employed for more than forty-five hours monthly. Additional protection for self-employed retirement-age workers is available under so-called Keogh plans, which permit the purchase of private pensions with a portion of before-tax income. In effect, this tax relief is similar to that available to wage and salary workers under qualified pension plans as a form of public subsidy of retirement benefits.

Health insurance coverage of self-employed workers is almost as comprehensive as retirement income coverage in most other industrialized countries. In part, this is because many of these countries have national health insurance programs with nearly universal coverage of families and individuals, regardless of the nature of their employment. In 1981, the European Economic Community called for universal coverage of sickness and maternity benefits, among other benefits, in its member countries, the intention being to establish uniformity (International Social Security Association 1981).

In the United States, only older self-employed workers are covered by the health insurance provisions of the Medicare program. Under increasingly restrictive limits, private health insurance premiums may qualify for deductions under federal and some state income tax laws. But for most workers, including the self-employed, this provides little or no benefit in meeting the costs of health insurance. Indeed, as a news report indicated,

obtaining health, disability, and even property insurance from private ven-
dors is likely to be expensive and time-consuming for the self-employed
(Berreby 1988).

As a general rule in the United States, the self-employed are excluded
from other types of protection against the risks of employment. Unemployment insurance benefits are exclusively for unemployed wage and salary
workers. Self-employed workers are not eligible for unemployment insurance benefits should their enterprises fail, though in some jurisdictions the
incorporated self-employed may receive benefits because of their classification as salaried workers. So it is with respect to hours of work, minimum
wage, and workers' compensation. Self-employment in the United States is
risky.

Industrial Homework

The recent growth in the United States of self-employment and work done
at home has raised legal issues surrounding the potential for exploitation of
de facto wage and salary workers. Individuals who can be established as
independent contractors, for example, are exempt from the provisions of the
federal wage and hour statute. Until recently, under that law, industrial
homework was forbidden in seven garment-related industries and in the
manufacture of costume jewelry. In December 1989, however, the federal
district court, District of Columbia, upheld an administrative ruling that
removed the ban in five of the seven industries.[10] If independent contractor
status can be established, homework is not prohibited, despite its potential
for exploitation.

Industrial homework appears to be on the increase, although data for earlier periods do not exist or are unreliable. The first comprehensive survey
of homework by the Bureau of Labor Statistics (Horvath 1986) reports that
17 million nonfarm workers did some paid work at home in May 1985,
almost an eightfold increase over the number reported in the 1980 census.
In 1985, a little more than half that number worked at home more than
eight hours per week. Only an estimated 1.3 million worked more than

---

10. Suit was brought by the International Ladies Garment Workers Union against the Sec-
retary of Labor protesting the removal of the ban on industrial homework. The union did not
appeal the decision. The five industries in which homework is now legally permitted include
gloves and mittens, handkerchiefs, buttons and buckles, embroidery, and some types of costume jewelry.

TABLE 5.3.   NONFARM SELF-EMPLOYMENT AND WORK AT HOME, MAY 1985 (in thousands)

	8 hours or more per week	35 hours or more per week	% full time
Total at-home employment	8,358	952	11.4
Self-employed	2,980	677	22.7
Incorporated	664	82	12.3
Unincorporated	2,316	595	25.7

SOURCE: Horvath 1986.

thirty-five hours per week. The majority of homeworkers were found to be men, but 60 percent more women than men put in a full workweek at home.

Of particular interest is the degree to which homework was reported as self-employment. More than one-third of those working at home for eight hours or more per week in May 1985 were reported as self-employed, but 71 percent of the full-time homeworkers were self-employed (table 5.3). The majority of self-employed homeworkers were unincorporated, including 60 percent of those engaged in professional services such as health and social services.

About half of home-based employment in May 1985 was in the service industries. The incorporated and unincorporated self-employed together accounted for about 36 percent of homework in that sector. The share of self-employment in services ranged from as much as 88 percent of personal services to 21 percent of professional services (table 5.4). The low rate in the professions probably results from the need of health practitioners and the legal profession to have resources at their disposal that cannot easily be accommodated in a home setting[11] (e.g., support staff).

Various technological, demographic, social, and political factors have encouraged the growth of homework. The personal computer, programmable knitting machines, and other electronic developments have increased the opportunity to work at home. So-called telecommuting has grown in such fields as insurance, finance, and communications (Chamot and Zalusky 1985; Gill 1985). For women, the lower cost of work-related expenses, especially child care, and flexibility in work scheduling have made work at

---

11. In the early decades of this century, as I recall from my own childhood, it was common for doctors to have their practice at home, though usually in premises separate from the rest of the household.

TABLE 5.4. SELF-EMPLOYMENT IN THE SERVICE INDUSTRIES, 1985
(in thousands)

| | Employed 8 hours or more | | % self-employed | | |
Services	Total	Self-employed	All	Incorporated	Unincorporated
All	4,132	1,479	35.7	4.6	31.1
Business and repair	679	424	62.4	9.8	52.6
Personal	428	376	87.8	1.6	86.2
Recreation, etc.	111	76	68.5	8.1	60.3
Professional	2,796	602	21.5	3.9	17.6

SOURCE: Horvath 1986.

home particularly attractive. The increased numbers of undocumented aliens may be another factor that has contributed to the growth of homework, since it may provide protection against authority as well as a livelihood. The deregulation movement and the lax enforcement of protective legislation are also contributing factors, exemplified by efforts during the Reagan administration to relax or void the rules against industrial homework.

In most instances of homework, particularly in the area of telecommuting, the employer-employee relationship has not been compromised. Nonetheless, efforts have been made to establish independent contractor status as a basis for exemption from protective legislation. This development could increase the possibilities for abuse and exploitation, leading to the return of the sweatshop, which the prohibitions on industrial homework were originally established to guard against. The homework issue has arisen not only in the traditional garment and related industries but also in newer electronically driven industries such as insurance and finance (Clutterbuck 1985). Telecommuting in the service industries has become a concern of unions, some of which fear abuse and whose organizational efforts would become more difficult with the growth of the "electronic cottage" (AFSCME 1984; Chamot and Zalusky 1985). Employers, by contrast, see in work at home the potential for savings in labor costs.

Thus far, the federal courts have upheld the very strict standards developed under wage-hour legislation to determine the legitimacy of claims by independent contractors. Those standards, which have been applied in other areas of protective legislation such as workers' compensation and unemployment insurance, restrict the degree of independent control over prices, location of facilities, advertising, ownership of equipment, and especially diversity of clientele[12] (Elisburg 1985). Until the recent relaxation of the ban on homework, the courts sustained those standards in a series of 1984 cases, including *Silent Woman v. Donovan, Donovan v. Dial America Marketing,* and *Donovan v. Darby Refining Co.*

Summary and Conclusions

Three areas of government intervention in the self-employment sector of the labor market were examined in this chapter. Two of these, support and regulation, mainly affect business enterprises. Self-employment and the self-employed are principally affected as an unintended concomitant of small business, the main target of the programs and regulations in these areas. Two exceptions are innovative programs established in other countries that provide unemployment insurance for unemployed wage and salary workers interested in becoming entrepreneurs and occupational licensing. Both of these developments are person-specific and, on that account, are more particularly aspects of the self-employed labor market.

Only in the third area, social protection, can one find recognition in public programs of the commonality of the self-employed and wage and salary workers. Provision under public programs for retirement income is found in most industrialized countries, including the United States. In many of these countries, the self-employed are also included in national health insurance programs.[13] This coverage probably results from a universalistic approach to meeting the health needs of the population, one that is different from the more selective approach taken in the United States. In other areas, such as unemployment and industrial accidents and disease, the self-employed individual in the United States is expected to bear the risks and costs.

If self-employment lies outside the ambit of explicit government labor market policies and programs in the United States, as this chapter indicates, should this continue to be the case? Should publicly supported programs that prepare individuals for self-employment become a significant feature of employment policy? Should occupational licensing be regulated so as to encourage more individuals to take up careers, perhaps as self-employed practitioners? Should the recognition of the self-employed as workers implied in the old-age pension program under Social Security be

---

12. Independent contractors who contract with only a single customer or client are suspected of colluding to avoid the requirements and costs of protective labor laws.

13. Should the United States adopt a national health plan, it will be interesting to see whether coverage of the self-employed will become an issue. That may depend on how the plan is financed, out of general revenues or by a payroll tax.

extended to other areas, such as training for and financing entry into self-employment, unemployment insurance, and workers' compensation?

The answers are not readily available, in part because of the paucity of research on self-employment as a labor market phenomenon. In the final chapter I will assess the role of self-employment in the labor market and the economy and propose a research agenda that may help us deal with this phenomenon as it relates to public policy.

CHAPTER SIX

Self-Employment and Labor Market Analysis

As a distinctive analytical category, self-employment has received virtually no attention in the study of labor markets. Few contemporary texts on the economics of labor, regardless of authorial viewpoint, make more than passing mention of the possibility that the study of self-employment may provide additional insight into the structure and behavior of labor markets. This disregard is understandable in part in that the decline of self-employment occurred largely before the establishment of industrial relations as a distinctive academic discipline.[1] Another explanation for the neglect can be found in the long-standing failure to distinguish between self-employment and small business enterprise. In fact, Alfred Marshall, a founder of modern economics, predicted the demise of both self-employment and small business because of his belief in the superior efficiency of large-scale, corporate business organizations (1898).

The material presented in the previous chapters underlines the contention that self-employment deserves explicit consideration as a labor market phenomenon. It has been shown that self-employment is an alternative to wage employment and that its reemergence is not a transitory phenomenon. More significantly, I have drawn comparisons between self-employed and wage and salary workers that serve to emphasize the labor market dimensions of self-employment, including relative earnings, gender and ethnic group

---

1. Labor relations textbooks that appeared in the first several decades of this century discuss self-employment as a facet of the producers cooperative movement. The vastly larger number of nonfarm self-employed at that period of U.S. economic development were simply ignored as outside the interest in labor-management relations.

differences in earnings and employment patterns, and certain institutional, especially government, aspects of self-employment. The review of the published data and limited body of literature on these relationships leads to the conclusion that treating self-employment as a vestigial form of business enterprise is no longer useful if we hope to understand more completely how labor markets work.

In this chapter I draw on the largely descriptive material of the earlier chapters to examine and appraise self-employment from a theoretical viewpoint as a labor market phenomenon. In chapters 2 and 3 particularly, efforts to explain employment and earnings observations were summarized but were not placed in a general framework of labor market analysis. This is the major objective of this chapter. With few exceptions, the substantive material of the earlier chapters will not be repeated.

The rebirth of self-employment has attracted some attention from the social sciences; studies have attempted to understand its role in a technologically advanced and, perhaps, maturing industrial economy. Steinmetz and Wright (1989), for example, have interpreted the rise in nonfarm self-employment as an anticapitalist development. Is self-employment such an ideological aberration, or does it have a significant place in the labor markets of the mainstream economy? As I have noted a number of times, the information base on which to establish conclusions in these matters is thin. Thus, I conclude with a research agenda that, if implemented, may reveal more about self-employment as a labor market phenomenon.

Fitting Self-Employment in Labor Market Theory

The standard model of the pricing and employment of labor services assumes a framework in which there are two distinctive functional groups, employer and employee, each with particular needs and objectives. The employer in this model (or, more impersonally, the firm) is an intermediary between suppliers of the factors required for production and the purchasers of the firm's output. The employer's principal interest is in maximizing the difference between the firm's revenues and its costs of production. To accomplish this, he or she must assume an active managerial and entrepreneurial role. The employees' interest, conversely, is in maximizing the return for their labor. Their role in the firm's profitability and survival is limited and relatively passive.

Does the combination of these functions in a single individual, the self-employed worker,[2] make a difference in theorizing about labor compensation? The earnings of a self-employed person depend not only on his or her skill and effort as a worker but also on how well he or she performs the managerial and entrepreneurial functions. When they are combined in a single individual, the two functions become complementary rather than competing, not only in the production of output but in the distribution of the firm's proceeds. Can labor market theory, under these conditions, help us to understand some of the more important observations described?

It may be useful to approach this issue by first examining the theoretical literature on producer cooperatives or worker-owned and worker-managed firms. Samplings of this literature are available in Vanek (1975) and Kennedy (1983). The interest of this literature is in knowing whether such firms would result in a more efficient allocation and use of resources and a general improvement in economic welfare, as compared with an economic system organized along capitalist lines. The latter is referred to by Meade (1972) as the entrepreneurial system, whereas worker-owned and worker-managed firms are referred to as the cooperative system. In Meade's basically neoclassical analysis, the difference between the two systems is that the worker-owned firm hires capital rather than labor. Although the operational rules are the same in both cases, the results in employment responses to changes in demand are sharply different. The other principal difference is in the distribution of the firm's surplus. Some authors conclude that because of the greater degree of distributional equity, productivity is increased as a result of the reduction in shirking and the release of workers' creativity (Meade 1972; Kennedy 1983).

Critics of the neoclassical approach to worker-owned cooperatives and employee stock ownership (e.g., Lichtenstein [1986], and Russell [1985]) object to its "black box" assumptions. They argue that, contrary to neoclassical values, interpersonal relations in a cooperative are important and that work has intrinsic as well as market value. A strong desire by workers for control over both the production process and the result are alleged to exist.

The applicability of this literature to self-employment seems limited, though some motivational aspects are analogous. But in all cases the as-

---

2. One might also consider employee-owned enterprises as analogous. But as I argue below, these are corporate bodies that, in most cases, maintain a functional distinction between managers and workers.

sumption is that the cooperative firm is a multiworker organization that must deal with external market environments and with internal relations among the worker-owners. Meade (1972), in fact, rejects the case of the single worker-owner or self-employed firm as useful in understanding the cooperative system because of the limitation of scale. Multiworker firms can expand, of course, by admitting new members, but the transformation of a self-employed worker into an employer-manager changes the meaning of self-employment that is currently used in conventional analysis. Whether such analysis, as embodied in modern labor market theory, can be helpful is explored below.

Supply Considerations

Theoretically, the supply side appears to be the easier case when examining the usefulness of the standard model of wage determination in understanding the economics of self-employment.[3] In the standard model, the firm meets its labor requirements from an external market in which it competes with other firms and workers compete similarly in their offers of labor services. For the self-employed individual in the economic short run, however, there is no external labor market. His or her sole source of labor is, so to speak, internal and defined within the relatively narrow limits imposed by human biology and intellect, on the one hand, and individual motivation and preferences, on the other.

Changes in the level of compensation for the self-employed worker, as for the worker employed by others, theoretically determine how much labor the self-employed individual is willing to offer. Since the self-employed are recruited mainly from the work force composed of paid employees, one may assume that the iso-utility maps of the self-employed are similar to those of wage workers and that their reactions to changes in wage rates would also be similar. Under these assumptions, other things being equal, the lower earnings of the self-employed ought to manifest themselves in relatively shorter weekly and annual hours. The actual situation, however, is in most cases contrary to this expectation. On average, as we have seen, compared

---

3. I am ignoring here the matter of the incentive to become self-employed but assume that the individual is already in that status. Most theoretical expositions argue that individuals will choose self-employment as the best alternative as long as its real wage is above that in other employments. Casson (1982), for example, argues that the supply of entrepreneurs is drawn from the pool of unemployed but selectively depending on the individual's belief in an invention or managerial ability and work-leisure preference.

with wage and salary workers, the self-employed work longer hours for relatively lower returns to their labor. Either the wage takes on a different meaning in self-employment or the "income effect" among the self-employed is much stronger than among otherwise comparable wage and salary workers.[4] Whichever inference is accepted, both suggest that the self-employed are different in their motivations and responses to market incentives.

Viewed as a firm, the self-employed individual appears to be a case of near-perfect inelasticity of labor supply, in which labor costs are variable within narrow limits in the short run.[5] At the limit of the self-employed firm's capacity, output can be increased only by adding capital or by employing others, which would also imply a change in scale and/or technology and, consequently, would represent a long- rather than a short-run response.

In principle, from a supply perspective, the long-run case seems compatible with the standard employer-employee model of labor compensation. The self-employed owner-worker can alter the firm's labor supply, short of hiring others, by improving the quality and productivity of his or her labor. With experience in managing the enterprise or with additional vocational training, the self-employed worker accumulates additional and/or more effective human capital. Consequently, because these developments have enlarged the firm's productive capacity, a larger market can be served. New or additional tools, as in the case of the conventional model, can also augment the supply of labor by increasing its productivity.

At some point, as Marshall long ago suggested (1898), it may become profitable to hire additional workers, thereby transforming self-employment into the conventional model of the business enterprise. In that case, of course, self-employment takes on a different meaning, with the managerial and administrative functions accounting for a much larger fraction of the individual's expenditure of labor. Boulier (1980) confirmed this in his study of self-employed dentists, finding that as prices for output (i.e., demand) rose, dentists tended to substitute other inputs in place of their own time.

---

4. An increase in hours of work offered as the real wage falls, according to the theory of the individual supply of labor, implies that the income effect dominates the substitution effect. If leisure is a normal good (i.e., can be substituted for consumption of goods and services), under the assumed decline in the real wage, leisure has become relatively more expensive and, therefore, less of it will be purchased and hours of work will either increase or not fall. For an excellent exposition of the theory of the individual supply of labor, see Ehrenberg and Smith (1991).

5. Assuming there are no other sources of income, labor in the case of self-employment is an overhead rather than a variable expense.

Demand Functions in Self-Employment

In a pure case of self-employment (i.e., the single-worker firm), the demand side seems less straightforward. The standard model posits a downward-sloping labor demand function resulting from the joint effect of diminishing physical returns and the behavior of product market prices. Although the demand for labor is a derived demand for the self-employed and for those employed by others, the concept of a production function does not seem useful in the case of a single-person firm. Since its labor supply is perfectly inelastic, no labor demand function can be derived by varying labor as a factor input. Of course, as the owner of capital, the self-employed worker would be concerned about its marginal productivity.

Further complications concerning labor demand in self-employment emerge as the product market is considered. If the self-employing firm is engaged in a market in which the product is homogeneous among all suppliers, the firm would be a price-taker. Price would need to cover only average total unit costs, including the worker's reservation wage and the costs of capital and materials. Few if any self-employed enterprises are engaged in such markets. Most, as in construction, the professions, and personal services, are providing nonhomogeneous services and products. Owner-operated taxicabs, automobile service stations, barbers, and beauty salons may more nearly approximate the homogeneous case, but even in these cases there is a substantial amount of product differentiation, real or imagined. Indirect evidence of the influence of product characteristics on self-employment was found by Leveson (1968) in his study of retail managers, in which self-employment rates increased with the degree of product heterogeneity. The imperfectly competitive product markets characteristic of self-employment may account for the greater degree of variability in the earnings of the self-employed compared with wage and salary workers.

The tentative conclusion suggested from the foregoing review is that labor market theory offers only a few insights into the compensation of self-employed workers. Factual observations tend for the most part to run counter to the hypotheses the theory provides. One suspects that the effects of scale may be critical in understanding the relative earnings of the self-employed. Labor in a single-person enterprise is a fixed cost, determined at a minimum by the subsistence needs of the individual and his or her family. Earnings depend, as they do for wage and salary workers, on the amount and quality of capital available and utilized. In the case of the self-employed worker, however, the capacity to utilize capital is limited by biological and technological factors. Earnings in self-employment depend on the individual's ability to deal with such constraints. Labor supply considerations, in fact, lead toward hypotheses differentiating the self-employed from wage and salary workers in their motivations and attitudes. Whether these alleged differences occur before or after self-employment is yet to be established empirically.

Nonpecuniary Determinants

Theoretically, entry into or exit from self-employment should conform to the general principles of occupational choice and worker mobility. Given freedom of choice, individuals become or do not become self-employed according to whether self-employment offers a higher level of utility than wage and salary employment. The decline of self-employment in earlier periods, when the earnings of the self-employed on average exceeded those of wage and salary workers, and the reemergence and growth of nonfarm self-employment during the more recent period, when average self-employment earnings fell well below those of wage and salary workers, seems to confound theoretical expectation. The latter development could be reconciled, however, under a broad concept of utility maximization that includes nonpecuniary as well as monetary components. Income from self-employment would then include nonmonetary satisfaction derived from the status of self-employment as well as a return from the individual's labor and ownership of physical capital. The review of the literature, especially chapters 2 and 3, points in this direction, highlighting the importance of changes in the demographic and social composition of self-employment and noting the more limited influence of broad economic developments on the growth of self-employment and trends in its relative earnings.

Various attempts have been made to uncover nonpecuniary elements in the labor market behavior of the self-employed. Most of these efforts are merely speculative or inconclusive in their findings. Phillips (1958), in his study of "little business," concluded that most of the self-employed are not utility maximizers, citing as evidence the lower rates of return from their labor and capital. Quinn (1980) adopted a similar position, denying that the utility functions of the self-employed were similar to those of wage and salary workers. Brock, Evans, and Phillips (1986) attempted without success to identify the presence of entrepreneurial ability as a trait that distinguishes the self-employed from wage workers. Eden (1975), by contrast, compared levels of job satisfaction between wage and salary workers and the self-employed and concluded that there was little difference. He also argued that the virtues of self-employment are probably overrated, given the higher degrees of financial risk and emotional investment. Nevertheless, Eden reported stronger positive attitudes toward autonomy and independence among the self-employed than among wage and salary workers. Fredland and Little (1985) reported increases in positive job attitudes among wage workers who switched to self-employment.[6] Such results, however, may reflect the individuals' attitudes toward their decision more than their attitude toward the self-employment experience itself.

Finally, I should sound a cautionary note about applying the neoclassical framework to the study of self-employment, or, for that matter, any labor market phenomenon. As several studies reviewed in earlier chapters make clear, the choice of self-employment may be governed by individual preferences as well as individual human and financial endowments. Those preferences and endowments, however, can be modified or have their direction altered by the institutional context; tax rates, minimum wages, or types of social protection, for example, may all have an effect.

Structural Factors in the Growth of Self-Employment

In chapter 2, I reviewed the literature on the growth of nonfarm self-employment that began in the 1970s. The strongest inference from that literature is that the self-employed act as rationally as other workers. Whether they respond to a cyclical downturn or to long-run economic and institutional developments, there is nothing from a purely behavioral viewpoint that distinguishes them from wage and salary workers. Most of the literature proposes that structural changes in the economy and its labor markets, which resulted in a loss of opportunities for wage employment, may have propelled the recent increase in self-employment. Most of these structural changes appear to be pulling individuals toward self-employment, however, rather than displacing them from wage and salary work. The growth of personal and business services, for example, has apparently created additional opportunities for self-employment.

Some labor force groups, in a broad sense, have been displaced from employment into self-employment. One might include individuals who turn

---

6. The same study also found that the switchers increased their hours of work and postponed retirement plans, both of which would be consistent with more positive job satisfaction.

to self-employment because of illness or disability. Other groups are forced into retirement or displaced by plant shutdowns and technological change, but these groups probably count for only a small fraction of the growth of self-employment. Thus broad structural changes in the economy do not seem to be driving the increase in self-employment. Wage and salary employment in the goods sector of the American economy has not increased in proportion to total employment, and job loss because of plant shutdowns and work force shrinkage has been largely concentrated in that sector, yet there is no evidence that workers are turning to self-employment for these reasons. Indeed, in their analysis of the increase in self-employment, Steinmetz and Wright (1989) show that the incidence of changes in self-employment by industry is quite varied even within the service sector. Proportionally, the largest *decreases* in self-employment rates in the 1970s were in such industries as medical and health services, eating and drinking establishments, and retailing. Substantially more modest decreases were registered in chemicals, machinery, and the metal industries. The largest gains in self-employment, according to their analysis, were in business services, construction, real estate, and professional services. It seems doubtful that workers displaced from the shrinking sectors are moving into the growth areas.

One other observation may be made in support of the hypothesis that the upturn in self-employment is being driven by "pull" factors. If job opportunities have been shrinking in the goods sector, especially in manufacturing industries, one would expect a marked demographic shift in the composition of the self-employed toward younger and newer entrants to the labor force. In fact, the average age of the self-employed has declined very little and continues to be substantially higher than that of the nonfarm labor force overall. The leading role of women in the increase in self-employment is also inconsistent with the displacement thesis. Since women have not been a major component of goods sector employment in the postwar era, the shrinkage of jobs in that sector is not a probable source of the increase in self-employment among women. Cohort effects may be involved, however, and this aspect needs further study.

One must remain uneasy about many such conclusions until the reemergence of self-employment has been explored more fully. In contrast with what is generally known about labor market change and behavior, there are too many anomalies and unanswered questions. Before turning to a proposed research agenda, I will attempt to explain our present understanding of the role of self-employment in the labor market.

The Labor Market Function of Self-Employment

From both a theoretical and a policy-making viewpoint, the question of self-employment as a rational response to changes in economic and institutional environments remains unanswered. Is the recent increase in self-employment an optimal allocation of labor in the U.S. economy? An affirmative answer has to contend with the alternative possibility that the increase is a response to labor market imperfections. In that empirical research has not addressed this question, it is possible to make a plausible case for either position.

A case for the market imperfection thesis may be implied from the nominally lower earnings of the self-employed compared with wage and salary earners. In a perfectly competitive labor market, given comparable human capital endowments and economic motivation, type of employment should have no effect on earnings. The self-employed sector of the labor market may be especially subject to imperfection because of the quality and cost of information. Underestimation of the capital required to sustain the enterprise beyond its infancy, overvaluation of one's managerial ability and experience, and insufficient knowledge of the product market may contribute to relatively poor earnings and high turnover in self-employment reflected, approximately, in high failure rates among small business.

In principle, removal of such barriers should both narrow the earnings gap between the self-employed and wage and salary workers and reduce the former's relative earnings. The conclusion by Evans and Leighton (1989), that the increase in self-employment has been led by workers more poorly equipped to compete in the wage labor market, implies that there is a group of noncompeting workers for whom self-employment is the best employment alternative. If such is the case, it is questionable from a public policy viewpoint to invest resources in self-employment training rather than in improving the competitive position of workers in wage employment.

By contrast, one can plausibly make the case that the low earnings in self-employment result not from imperfect information and underinvestment in human capital but from rational calculation and action based on the diversity of interests and abilities in the labor force. Such a case rests on the assumption that individuals have accurate knowledge not only of their preferences and physical and intellectual endowments but also of the product market. Self-employment, in Quinn's phrase, is for such individuals a "career option." The low earnings may represent a trade-off for greater autonomy in one's work and in the use and returns from capital, flexibility in allocating time between market and nonmarket activities, and so on.

On a less abstract plane, as earlier chapters suggest, the role of self-employment may be to extend the range of options for participation in the labor market and, on that account, serve to increase the ability of the labor force to adapt to economic and industrial change. In some instances, such as some of the professions, where interpersonal contact between a client and a specialist is required, self-employment may be the most efficient means of providing services. The opportunity to develop an idea free of the constraints and distraction of a wage job is another positive role. Self-employment may also provide a kind of "shock absorber" function. Some individuals displaced from paid employment by plant shutdowns, technological obsolescence, ill health, or mandatory retirement have turned to self-employment as a means of continuing income and/or maintaining self-esteem. Individuals handicapped by their language abilities, as in the case of immigrants, or discriminated against because of race or gender have used self-employment as a means of earning a living. Increasing the range of ways of making a living in the labor market either as a transitional part of the work life cycle or as a permanent career may be as important in a democratic society as whether such choices are economically efficient.

Research Agenda

Every topic addressed in this book has revealed a number of unanswered questions relevant to understanding the behavior, role, and public policy implications of self-employment. Several studies have called attention to the gaps in information and understanding and have proposed topics for additional research (Evans and Leighton 1987, 1989; Steinmetz and Wright 1989). In this concluding section, I propose five areas for such research. One is the development of a more adequate data base. The others concern the study of the behavior of self-employment under varying economic and labor market conditions; the movement into and out of self-employment as a form of occupational choice and/or occupational mobility; the earnings differentials between self-employed and wage and salary workers and among various self-employed groups; and the influence of institutional factors on these areas, including the effects of public policies and programs.

DATA SOURCES AND NEEDS

The appendix describes the principal sources of data that have been used in studies of self-employment: the decennial censuses of population and the Current Population Survey, both of which provide data on the demographic, social, and occupational characteristics of workers. Data on the self-employed in these categories are accessible by computer. But even so, their usefulness for analysis of the dynamics of self-employment is limited. CPS data on self-employment (i.e., class of worker) is reported only once annually, as is establishment data from the reports of the Social Security Administration and the Internal Revenue Service. The influence of cohort effects on longer-term analysis increases, of course, with the length of the interval between observations in such data sets. It would be desirable, thus, to have more frequent observation and more detail relevant to labor market behavior and issues.

Longitudinal or panel data would help in understanding the course of self-employment. Studies from which I have drawn data and/or findings have used longitudinal data sources but have ignored potentially rewarding areas and other data sources. The National Longitudinal Survey data were used by Fredland and Little (1981, 1985) and by Evans and Leighton (1987, 1989). In each of these studies, however, the authors were interested in particular demographic groups. Indeed, the NLS data omit panel data on some groups with a greater likelihood of self-employment. Quinn (1980) and Fuchs (1982) utilized the Retirement History Survey but limited their analysis to men. The Continuous Work History sample survey of Social Security participants has not ever been used, nor, from the evidence, has the Michigan Panel Study of Income Dynamics.

As mentioned, one common difficulty for researchers in the field is the lack of uniformity in the definition of self-employment. I have attempted, with only partial success, to confine my observations to those self-employed who do not employ others. The self-employed who do employ others are of interest but should be identified as a separate category, in the same way the incorporated self-employed are. Some studies do not make this distinction; others include unpaid family workers and/or partners as self-employed.

There is sufficient difference among these groups in their demographic characteristics, earnings and employment, and motivation to urge that data sources provide detail sufficient for both analysis of such differences and comparability across data sources. Data bases that provide information on personal and social characteristics should include gender as a major category so as to enable the growing participation of women in self-employment to be analyzed.

I have found a number of establishment data bases useful in identifying broad tendencies in the industrial distribution and earnings of the self-employed. Except for the Social Security payroll and income tax reports, however, these sources do not specifically distinguish between wage and salary workers and the self-employed. IRS data, economic censuses, and their information on business enterprises owned by minorities and women, based as they are on legal form of organization rather than class of worker, provide limited knowledge of self-employment as such. The same is true of the Small Business Data Base developed by the Office of Advocacy of the Small Business Administration.[7]

Establishment data bases should be continued and regularly enhanced if possible by identifying the gender and racial characteristics of business owners, as has been done to this point on a sporadic basis. Current Population Survey data on self-employment, now recorded on an annual basis, should be recorded quarterly and contain greater detail on industry and occupational information as well as demographic and social characteristics.[8] The CPS would then become the principal source for the analysis of differences in labor market participation by class of worker. Finally, the definitions used in longitudinal data bases should be brought into conformity with those of the CPS to increase their value for analysis.

BEHAVIOR OF NONFARM SELF-EMPLOYMENT

The process and factors involved in the transformation of self-employment from a declining to an advancing sector of the labor market need more penetrating analysis than has been undertaken to date. We lack a satisfactory accounting of the extent to which this recent development has been due to structural changes and the extent to which it is simply a result of short-run business cycles. Since the two types of change can occur together, it would be useful to sort out their relative influence on self-employment. Only two studies (Blau 1987; Steinmetz and Wright 1989) have been directly concerned with the growth in self-employment in the 1970s. Steinmetz and Wright, though concerned with changes in social class structure, address some of the macroeconomic concerns of interest to labor economists as well.

---

7. Because the Small Business Data Base is derived from Dun and Bradstreet files, it excludes firms without employees and that have had no credit check (Lichtenstein 1989). Such a restriction probably excludes a majority of the self-employed.

8. For example, the sample survey should distinguish self-employed who work at home from those whose business premises are elsewhere. Such detail would be useful not only in analysis but because of its public policy implications.

Prior to these studies, the most popular explanation for the growth of nonfarm self-employment was what may be called the "rising tide" hypothesis: the growth of industries that have relatively large proportions of self-employment, notably the service industries, increases the overall importance of self-employment (Fuchs 1968; Stanback 1979; Solomon 1986). In these studies, the growth of self-employment was an incidental aspect rather than the focus of the analysis.

The validity of the rising tide hypothesis is weakened by evidence from more recent studies. Blau (1987), in one of the few direct treatments of the increase in self-employment, found evidence that intersectoral differences in total factor productivity as a proxy for technological change contributed to the recent upturn. That study did not, however, disaggregate within sectors. Tschetter (1987) found a higher rate of increase in self-employment in producers and business services than elsewhere, but that study was not primarily directed to the issue of overall employment growth. Only one study to date (Steinmetz and Wright 1989) distinguishes between inter- and intrasectoral changes in self-employment rates. Though its findings require further analysis, they nevertheless strongly suggest that the rise in self-employment is more than a case of differential growth between sectors. A corollary of the intersectoral shift hypothesis is that the shrinkage of jobs in the goods sectors displaces both older workers and new entrants to the labor force. Mobility studies that identify both the labor force status and industrial and occupational origins of persons entering self-employment would be extremely helpful in understanding the growth of self-employment.

There is no record of the exact timing of these changes. Were the rising tide hypothesis correct, it would be difficult to explain why self-employment before the 1970s was declining while overall employment in the service sector was increasing.

Research on the influence of business cycles on self-employment is unsatisfactory. Reference was made in chapter 2 to several studies that find support for a positive relationship between the overall rate of unemployment and changes in the rate of self-employment. Since the bulk of the increase in self-employment has occurred in the service industries, these studies suggest a greater degree of cyclical sensitivity in that sector than is generally believed to be the case. Although not concerned with the business cycle, Fuchs (1968) found that service sector stability may be due to the presence of relatively large numbers of self-employed workers. His analysis indicated that nonfarm self-employment exhibited the smallest deviation from trend—.01 percent compared with 6.4 percent for total nonfarm employment during the 1947–65 period. Clearly, this finding runs counter to a cyclical explanation.

A probable hypothesis from such observations would be that the self-employed, because they are unhampered by institutional restraints, such as a collective agreement, and because their capital is at risk, are more willing and able than wage and salary workers to adjust the price of their labor and so remain employed. Covick (1983), as noted earlier, also suggests that increases in self-employment may be a form of underemployment. This possibility is also suggested in an OECD survey (1986), but again it is not supported by empirical investigation. The OECD study, based on the experience in its member countries, concluded that self-employment is probably cyclically neutral across countries. In a time-series analysis of experience in the United States between 1947 and 1985, Steinmetz and Wright (1989) found evidence for a countercyclical effect, but this effect declined over the period. The cyclical behavior of self-employment in other countries with a history of business cycles would be a worthy and interesting topic to pursue.

The differences in the results and conclusions of studies on the relative importance of cyclical and structural influences on the rate of self-employment clearly point to the need for a change in research focus. Most of the studies to which I have thus far referred have employed rather broad industrial and occupational or macro-level categories. An approach that is disaggregated with respect to industries and labor markets might be more rewarding. Most self-employment serves local markets and, correspondingly, is more likely to be affected by local labor market conditions than by national developments. No study I have examined has taken this into account.

MOBILITY AND OCCUPATIONAL CHOICE AMONG THE SELF-EMPLOYED

A necessary complement to studies on the overall behavior and growth of self-employment would be a study of entry into and exit from self-employment. Such movements, as noted, are a form of labor mobility, but they also frequently involve occupational choice and change. Because there are marked demographic and social differences between the self-employed and paid employees, and among the self-employed themselves, there is a need to identify how these differences develop as end results and how they change in varying environments. The central issue might be whether the two types of employment share a common labor market.

To this end, two general research approaches could be pursued. One would be to test for the presence of a segmented labor market in which institutional as well as social and cultural influences bear on the choice of self-employment. The underrepresentation in self-employment of women and racial and ethnic minorities suggests barriers to entry, rather than a protective market environment, as some studies have hypothesized and for which they have found some support.

The alternative approach would be to explore factors affecting or responsive to human capital differences, such as previous work experience, technical and skills training, and some measure of managerial ability. Evans and Leighton (1989), who looked at such factors, could find no significant relationship between previous experience in wage employment and entry into self-employment. Blau (1985), in his study of self-employment in an underdeveloped economy, utilized the dual labor market approach, but its applicability to an advanced industrialized economy has yet to be tested. Borjas and Bronars (1989) combined both approaches in their study of consumer discrimination and the self-employment decision. That study, however, was confined to racial and ethnic differences among males. Clearly, broader studies embracing other demographic and social groups and a wider spectrum of occupations and industries would help further the understanding of self-employment as an occupational choice.

In particular, I would urge more intensive study of women and self-employment. What are the forces that have led or driven the dramatic increase in self-employment among women? Why are their earnings, even when adjusted for time worked, education, and so on, so much lower than those of women in wage jobs, let alone men in general? What are the family statuses of self-employed women: do they have children, other sources of income, including other household members, and so forth? Such studies ought to have a high priority in a labor market research program.

EARNINGS DIFFERENCES

Prior to the recent growth of nonfarm self-employment, interest in the earnings of the self-employed was either incidental or subordinate to other research interests. Efforts to estimate the contribution of self-employment to national income are an example of this trend (Feinstein 1968; Rasmussen 1968). This apparent disinterest survives in more recent efforts to understand the so-called underground economy. Leveson's study (1968), by contrast, though part of a broader study of the service industries, was among the first to notice and attempt to understand earnings differences between salaried and self-employed workers.

The analysis of earnings differences is hampered by the lack of reliable earnings measures. Reported earnings in self-employment are believed to suffer from three difficulties. First, there is the difficulty of separating labor income from the return from capital and other property income. Second, there is the propensity to underreport income for tax purposes. Third, record keeping among the self-employed may not be as accurate as that of larger enterprises, simply because the self-employed often lack the resources both to keep accounts and serve the market. The more self-employed workers and small businesses are exempt from regulation, and thus relieved from certain obligations to keep accurate records, the more likely measurement of their labor incomes will continue to fall short of a desirable standard.

I offer no specific remedy for improving the measurement of earnings in self-employment. Initial efforts, however, should be directed at discovering how serious the problem is. Again, it would be useful not only to make an overall assessment of the measurement gap but also to establish how this gap varies with demographic and market characteristics. Such research should not inhibit additional study of the determinants of the earnings of the self-employed, especially as compared with those of paid employees. It is difficult to believe that measurement error alone can account for the major portion of the differences between the two groups.

Studies of earnings differences between wage and salary work and self-employment and within self-employment itself need to cover a broader range of labor market participants. Most studies thus far have focused on particular groups, selected in part because of the accessibility of data. Brock, Evans, and Phillips (1986) and Evans and Leighton (1989), for example, based their earnings analyses on males, on white males in the latter case. Although Evans and Leighton acknowledged the growing importance of women in self-employment in their 1987 study, no published study thus far has attempted to analyze the apparently striking earnings differences between self-employed women and other demographic and social groups. Nor has serious study been made of the effect of self-employment on the earnings of minority groups, especially blacks, though race has been entered in a few cases as an independent variable in the overall analysis of self-employment earnings.

Almost any question that might be asked about earnings differences generally could also be asked about the earnings of the self-employed. Several issues have emerged from the literature that are of particular interest. Evans and Leighton (1989) concluded that the lower earnings of the self-employed represent a sorting process. Compared with wage and salary workers, the self-employed are disproportionately less productive than their employee counterparts because of their lower-quality human capital endowments or other disadvantages, however imposed. For such individuals, therefore, self-employment is the best alternative use of their resources. As earlier discussion indicates, this speculation needs to be challenged by further empirical study.

Measured by their relative dispersion, earnings in self-employment have a much greater range than is commonly found in the earnings of wage and salary workers. Furthermore, the apparent earnings disadvantage of the self-employed seems paradoxical. Theoretically, earnings variability is associated with a greater propensity to bear risk, as in small business. Their lower earnings, on the face of it, suggest that the self-employed may not be fully compensated for risk-taking. There is the possibility, however, that the self-employed are not risk-takers and may in fact have an above-average degree of aversion, as Taubman (1975) concludes in one of the few studies to touch on this question.

How important are nonmonetary components of compensation in accounting for earnings differentials? This issue, which is especially germane to the relatively lower earnings of self-employed women, remains unresolved with respect to the differences between paid workers and the self-employed. Studies of physicians (Kehrer 1976; Bobula 1980), after adjusting for differences in medical specialties and time worked, found that women earned less than men but that employee status tended to raise the relative earnings of women physicians. Are self-employed women being compensated in part by nonmonetary income, such as having more time with their children during their formative years? Do women physicians and, indeed, self-employed women in general sort themselves into lower-paying employments because of such compensation? Or are they in these jobs because of discrimination on the part of training and financial institutions?

INSTITUTIONAL INFLUENCES ON SELF-EMPLOYMENT

In earlier chapters, institutional influences on entry into or barriers to self-employment were described. Two studies, for example, included the impact of marginal rates of income taxation in their analysis of the rise in nonfarm self-employment (Blau 1987; Evans and Leighton 1987). The statutory minimum wage (Blau 1987; Covick 1983), Social Security, education and skills training, and retirement policies are other such influences that have been tested for their impact on self-employment rates and, in some cases, the earnings of the self-employed. The findings are by no means definitive nor do they adequately cover the ground. No study, to my knowledge, has explored the effects of occupational licensing on the choice between self-employment and paid-employee status. If the protection from competitive pressure afforded by such licensing were removed or weakened, would this encourage or discourage self-employment? On a broader level, the effect of the deregulation movement, as manifested in the various exemptions for small business, also remains unexplored.

Programs that support self-employment and small business should be monitored. The experiments abroad and, more recently, in the United States that use unemployment insurance as a form of venture capital and the proposals to encourage self-employment among low-income workers as a form of on-the-job training and skills development may, as suggested by Balkin (1989), be areas deserving of study. The federal and state governments' small business lending and procurement programs, especially those directed to encouraging business ownership among women and disadvantaged minorities, are another area in which additional evaluation studies would be worthwhile.

RESEARCH ON MOTIVATION

The choice of employment, whether constrained or relatively free, implies underlying behavioral influences. Not all individuals with similar demographic, social, and occupational profiles necessarily respond in like ways to market and other external influences on employment choice. At the microeconomic level, studies of the choice of self-employment and of the labor market behavior of the self-employed remain largely theoretical and/or speculative. Evans and Leighton (1987) found in their review of economic theories of entrepreneurship that there was an emphasis on self-selection derived from self-recognition of managerial or entrepreneurial ability and on relatively low levels of risk aversion. According to this theory, individuals who lack such traits become wage workers *ab initio* or after failure to survive in their own business. Borjas and Bronars (1989) found evidence that self-selection was a differentiating response to consumer discrimination. Further development of this approach may prove fruitful in understanding the motivation to become self-employed.

Some behavioral scientists have also attempted to discover the traits and cultural values that distinguish small business owners from those who work for others. McClelland's achievement need has been proposed as one motivator, but it is not clear why or how this varies among individuals. Scase and Goffee (1982) and others suggest that a desire for autonomy and an interest in upward social mobility (i.e., from blue-collar manual worker to petit bourgeois) are motivating factors. The measurement of such traits and values, especially in a predictive way, has not been successfully accomplished, however.

In addition, it is questionable whether the self-employed and small business owners are truly entrepreneurial in the sense conceived by Knight (1933) and Schumpeter (1934). Scase and Goffee (1982) in their case study of twenty-five male sole proprietors and their wives found that a majority had been forced by redundancy or dissatisfaction in their wage jobs to take up self-employment. The desire for independence was latent, apparently, until circumstances forced the choice. Significantly, most of this group had no interest in expanding their enterprises or employing persons outside the household. Further and more representative studies would be helpful in distinguishing entrepreneurs in the classical sense from those who view self-employment as essentially no different from paid employment.

Conclusion

The study of self-employment as a labor market phenomenon is clearly at an early, perhaps only an incipient, stage. Researchers in this area must be willing to face severe problems of data availability and ambiguity and be prepared to develop a theoretical framework capable of generating testable hypotheses appropriate to those characteristics of self-employment that may distinguish it from wage and salary employment. Those who conduct research in this area may find that the reward derived from furthering the understanding of diversity in labor markets is substantial.

Appendix

Counting the Self-Employed

It has long been the practice, in the major published sources at least, to relegate self-employment to a secondary position, usually without the detail essential to understanding its labor market features. Indeed, until the 1940 census self-employment was not distinguished from other types of employment. Despite improvements in labor force measurement and the addition of sources of data, it is often difficult to find information in requisite detail.[1] All the sources, for one reason or another, fall short. Nevertheless, it may be helpful to describe the sources that are available and to comment on their respective features, desirable and otherwise.

Information on the self-employed can be found in a number of places, but primarily government publications. These documents, both in published and unpublished form, vary in their levels of descriptive and analytical accessibility. Although the line between household and establishment data sources is somewhat blurred, it is convenient to divide the discussion into these two categories.

The principal household data sources are the decennial census and the monthly report on the labor force derived from the Current Population Survey. These two sources provide the longest series of data on self-employment, dating back to the 1940 census and the initiation of the Monthly Report on the Labor Force. In published form, both sources offer limited information on nonfarm self-employment. The censuses since 1940, for instance, have not been consistent in the kind and level of detail pro-

---

1. The limited amount of published data on self-employment is not unique to the United States. Data sources for most other countries (e.g., Australia) suffer from the same deficiency (Burgess 1988).

137

vided. Published CPS data (annual averages are found in the January issues of *Employment and Earnings,* published by the Department of Labor, Bureau of Labor Statistics) provide breakdowns by two-digit industry and by sex and race. Additional detail from both sources are available from the public-use tapes (Becker 1984; Blau 1987; Evans and Leighton 1987). Also useful is the historical series constructed by Lebergott (1964), who interpolated census data back to 1900. This series includes the distribution of non-farm self-employment by broad industry groups and is designed to be compatible with Current Population Survey labor force definitions.

Other household-based data sources include the National Longitudinal Survey, which permits cohort analysis of the dynamics of labor market behavior, though its panel data on women are for age groups less likely to be self-employed; the University of Michigan Panel Study of Income Dynamics; and the recently established Bureau of the Census Survey of Income and Program Participation (SIPP). The first two sources allow cohort analysis over relatively long periods of time. The SIPP follows a cohort for a period of two and one-half years.[2]

None of the establishment-based data sources provides for cohort analysis. Nevertheless, they contain useful information and to some degree serve as a check on other sources. Two of these sources have been helpful in this study: the sample data on workers covered under the Old-Age, Survivors, Disability and Health Insurance (OASDHI) programs and the individual income tax returns of persons reporting as sole proprietors. Data on the Social Security program are reported in the annual statistical supplement to the *Social Security Bulletin,* published by the U.S. Department of Health and Human Services. Internal Revenue Service data are reported annually in the *Statistics of Income Bulletin: Sole Proprietors.* The Social Security data provide breakdowns by sex and age; total and taxable earnings are also reported. IRS data are based on tax returns and do not necessarily represent an equivalent number of persons, but they do provide a breakdown by industry at the three-digit level. For several years, sole proprietors were also identified by gender, but this was discontinued after 1977. Other data in this source include business receipts and business expenses, from which a rough calculation of the proprietors' labor income can be derived.

---

2. For a brief description of this data source and comparison with the Current Population Survey, see Haber, Lamas, and Lichtenstein 1987. A somewhat more technical description can be found in U.S. Department of Health and Human Services, *Social Security Bulletin, Annual Statistical Supplement, 1988.*

Under the sponsorship of the Small Business Administration, a Small Business Data Base (SBDB) has been developed from data supplied through the Dun and Bradstreet credit-rating program and refined for analytical use. Four files, including a longitudinal establishment file, provide information intended mainly for policy analysis by the Small Business Administration. Further information on this data source can be found in the *State of Small Business, 1985*. Self-employed individuals are not identified as such in this source, however.

Additional establishment data on sole proprietorships are found in all but one of the quinquennial economic censuses. These include the censuses of the wholesale and retail trades and of the service industries. Each of these contains data at the four-digit level on the number of establishments, sales, payrolls, and employment by legal form of organization. It is thus possible to estimate by detailed industry the number of establishments in the category of sole proprietorships, to know whether they employ others, and to trace over time their relationship with other forms of business organizations.

For various administrative and technical reasons, the numbers of individuals classified as self-employed cannot be strictly compared across the data sources. The CPS counts individuals only once, according to their principal employment activity or source of labor income. Since the data are recorded only once a year (usually in March), it does not necessarily correspond with the individual's employment during the balance of the year.[3] For similar reasons, both Social Security and IRS data may overcount the numbers included in any employment category. Individuals who were both wage and salary workers and self-employed in the reporting year are counted in both categories in the Social Security records. Thus, in 1980, according to the CPS, there were 6,850 nonfarm self-employed, while according to the Social Security count there were 8,200 such individuals in the same year. On the one hand, the IRS data on sole proprietors overcounts, because all such enterprises for which a tax return is filed in a given year are counted, both those operating during the entire year and those established at any time during the same period.[4] On the other hand, the numbers of self-employed

---

3. Comparison of self-employment rates based on the individual's status in March and on the longest job during the preceding twelve-month period show some difference in level and trend in the postwar period.

4. At the same time, there is reason to believe that the unduplicated numbers of self-employed may be underrepresented in these sources because of the opportunity to avoid income and self-employment taxes afforded by self-employment. See the discussion below.

TABLE A-1   NONFARM SELF-EMPLOYMENT, MAY 1983 (in thousands)

Employment category	Number	%	% of total
All categories	12,950	100.0	13.5
Unincorporated	7,482	58.0	7.8
Incorporated	2,590	20.0	2.7
Wage and salary moonlighters	2,878	22.0	3.0

SOURCE: SBA, *State of Small Business,1986.*

from both these sources are undoubtedly underreported, because of the well-known propensity of the self-employed and small businesses to evade taxes.[5]

In addition, the definition of self-employment varies from one source to another. In the CPS and Census counts since 1967, individuals who are in a legal sense employees of their own corporations are counted as wage and salary workers. Such individuals can be identified by manipulation of the tape source but generally are not so identified in routine published sources. (The 1970 census is an exception.) CPS data do not distinguish partners from other types of self-employed workers, while the quinquennial business censuses show partnerships as a separate category. IRS data also treat partnerships as a separate classification. CPS data, even in tape form, provide too little information about so-called moonlighters (i.e., persons holding wage and salary jobs who are also engaged in their own businesses). The complexity of the self-employed status is illustrated in table A-1.

Questions about the degree of independence of some individuals reported in these and other sources as self-employed can affect the reliability of the employment measures. Franchising and the revival of some forms of industrial homework, for example (the latter is discussed in chapter 5 in the context of government and self-employment), cast doubt in some cases on the degree of autonomy involved. Several studies (Elfring 1988; Lozano 1989) have suggested that some possibly substantial number of individuals are not truly self-employed because they serve only a single client. To date, however, such instances cannot be easily disentangled except on a case-by-case basis. By contrast, self-employed who have incorporated are classified in official statistics as employees of their own corporation (table A-1). Be-

5. Discussion with personnel responsible for the Social Security data, for example, indicates that there is no estimate of the numbers legally subject to the self-employment tax who fail to file the tax return.

cause of varying definitions and reliability of the reporting, then, estimates of self-employment and its associated characteristics may be either under- or overestimated.

Panel data referred to earlier have their own special problems. The age-sex cohorts that constitute the National Longitudinal Survey panels do not include all age groups, for example. In addition, panel data are subject to attrition, so that the group surviving at the end of the period of observation may be different in important ways from the initial sample.

Although the foregoing considerations suggest caution in using data on the extent and nature of self-employment, perhaps the most intensely debated issue concerns the so-called underground economy, around which a small industry has developed. Some view the growth of the hidden economy and of self-employment in general as the result of structural changes in industrial economies (Mattera 1985). Interest in the phenomenon, particularly among economists, has been motivated primarily by concern over tax evasion and secondarily over the accuracy of national income and product accounts. This interest has led to international scholarly conferences (Gaertner and Wenig 1985) and government studies (U.S. General Accounting Office 1981; Carson 1984; Organization for Economic Cooperation and Development 1986), as well as to numerous private investigations (Henry 1981; Mattera 1985; O'Higgins 1985; Simon and Witte 1982; Smith 1986; Alessandrini and Dallago 1987).

For the study of self-employment as a labor market phenomenon, the critical concerns are the numbers of self-employed workers engaged in "off-the-books" enterprises and the reliability of reported earnings. Estimates of these figures vary widely. Feige (1979) and Gutmann (1979), though approaching the phenomenon from different methodological viewpoints, concluded that large numbers of people participate in off-the-books work, while others (McCrohan and Smith 1983; McDonald 1984; Evans and Leighton 1989) have concluded that the numbers officially reported as self-employed are close to the true numbers.

Estimates of unreported income likewise range widely, from 3 to 33 percent of gross national product according to the studies Carson (1984) reviewed. There are no acceptable data that would permit a reliable adjustment of reported earnings, though one study (U.S. General Accounting Office 1981) found that the discrepancy between reported and actual earnings decreased with the level of income or earnings. It is clear, however, that the self-employed have the largest propensity and best opportunity for underreporting taxable income. The IRS study estimated that only 60 to 65 percent of all self-employment income was reported in 1981 (Simon and Witte 1982). Carson (1984) reports that one-fourth of total unreported legally derived income was accounted for by nonfarm sole proprietors; for that class of worker, only 41 percent of income was voluntarily reported, compared with 94 percent for wage and salary workers. The General Accounting Office exact match study of income reporting found that 16 percent of individuals identified in the Current Population Survey as self-employed did not report taxable income to either the IRS or the Social Security Administration. Given the virtual impossibility of estimating the extent of unreported income on a basis that also identifies demographic and labor market characteristics, one has to qualify statements about earnings variations by pointing to their source of bias or remove from a data source those individuals whose earnings records are ambiguous, as at least one study has done (Evans and Leighton 1989).

References

AFSCME. 1984. *Collective Bargaining Reporter*. No. 24. Washington, D.C.: AFSCME.

Alessandrini, Sergio, and Bruno Dallago, eds. 1987. *The Unofficial Economy*. Aldershot, Eng.: Gower.

Allen, David, and Amanda Hunn. 1985. "An Evaluation of the Enterprise Allowance Scheme." *Employment Gazette* 93 (August): 313–17.

American Bar Foundation. 1985. *The Lawyer Statistical Report, 1984*. Chicago: American Bar Foundation.

———. 1986. *Supplement to the Lawyer Statistical Report: The U.S. Legal Profession in 1985*. Chicago: American Bar Foundation.

American Dental Association. 1969. *The 1968 Survey of Dental Practice*. Chicago: American Dental Association.

———. 1983. *The 1982 Survey of Dental Practice*. Chicago: American Dental Association.

———. 1987. *The 1986 Survey of Dental Practice*. Chicago: American Dental Association.

American Medical Association. Center for Health Policy Research. 1984. *Socioeconomic Characteristics of Medical Practice, 1984*. Chicago: American Medical Association.

American Medical Association. Center for Health Services Research and Development. 1980. *Profile of Medical Practice, 1980*. Chicago: American Medical Association.

Ando, Faith. 1986. "An Analysis of the Formation and Failure Rates of Minority-Owned Firms." *Review of Black Political Economy* 15 (Fall): 51–72.

Anspach, William N., and Robert M. Snider. 1984. "The Professional Corporation: Is It Dead?" *Practical Accountant* 17 (January): 24–33.

Aram, John D., and Jeffrey S. Coomes. 1985. "Public Policy and the Small Business Sector." *Policy Studies Journal* 13 (June): 692–700.

Balkin, Steven. 1988. "Self-Employment Assistance Programs in the United States Targeted to Low-Income Disadvantaged People." In *Proceedings of the Fortieth Annual Meeting of the Industrial Relations Research Association*, 356–63. Madison, Wisc.: Industrial Relations Research Association.

————. 1989. *Self-Employment for Low-Income People.* New York: Praeger.

Bauman, Kurt. 1988. "Characteristics of the Low-Income Self-Employed." In *Proceedings of the Fortieth Annual Meeting of the Industrial Relations Research Association,* 339–45. Madison, Wisc.: Industrial Relations Research Association.

Bearse, Peter J., 1984. "An Econometric Analysis of Black Entrepreneurship." *Review of Black Political Economy* 12 (Spring): 117–34.

Becker, Eugene. 1984. "Self-Employed Workers: An Update to 1983." *Monthly Labor Review* 107 (July): 14–18.

Bendick, Marc, Jr., and Mary Lou Egan. 1987. "Transfer Payment Diversion for Small Business Development: British and French Experience." *Industrial and Labor Relations Review* 40 (July): 528–42.

Ben-Porath, Yoram. 1986. "Self-Employed and Wage Earners in Israel: Findings from the Census of Population 1972," Research Paper 187. In *Studies in the Population of Israel,* ed. Usiel Smelz and Gad Nathan. Jerusalem: Magnes Press.

Berlant, Jeffrey L. 1975. *Profession and Monopoly.* Berkeley: University of California Press.

Berney, Robert E., and Ed Owens. 1985. "A Theoretical Framework for Small Business Policy." *Policy Studies Journal* 13 (June): 681–91.

Berreby, David. 1988. "Getting Insurance When Self-Employed." *New York Times,* November 20.

Birch, David, and Colin Gallagher. n.d. "The Wellsprings of Work: The U.S. and the U.K." Typescript.

Birch, David, and Susan MacCracken. 1985. "The Small Business Share of Job Creation: Lessons Learned from the Use of a Longitudinal File." MIT Program on Neighborhood and Regional Change. Mimeo.

Bishop, John H. 1987. "American Job Growth: What Explains It?"*Portfolio: International Economic Perspectives* 12.

Blair, Roger D., and Stephen Rubin, eds. 1980. *Regulating the Professions.* Lexington, Mass.: Lexington Books.

Blau, David M. 1985. "Self-Employment and Self-Selection in Developing Country Labor Markets." *Southern Economic Journal* 52 (October): 351–63.

————. 1987. "A Time-Series Analysis of Self-Employment in the United States." *Journal of Political Economy* 95 (June): 445–67.

Blau, Francine D., and Marianne A. Ferber. 1986. *The Economics of Women, Men, and Work.* Englewood Cliffs, N.J.: Prentice-Hall.

Blaustein, Albert P., and Charles O. Porter. 1954. *The American Lawyer.* Chicago: University of Chicago Press.

Bobula, Joel D. 1980. "Income Differences between Male and Female Physicians." In *Profile of Medical Practice, 1980,* 123–33. Chicago: American Medical Association.

Borjas, George J. 1985. "Assimilation, Changes in Cohort Quality, and the Earnings of Immigrants." *Journal of Labor Economics* 3 (October): 463–89.

————. 1986. "The Self-Employment Experience of Immigrants." *Journal of Human Resources* 21 (Fall): 485–506.

Borjas, George J., and Stephen G. Bronars. 1989. "Consumer Discrimination and Self-Employment." *Journal of Political Economy* 97: 581–605.

Boulier, Bryan L. 1980. "An Empirical Examination of the Influence of Licensure and Licensure Reform on the Geographical Distribution of Dentists." In *Occupational Licensure and Regulation,* ed. Simon Rottenberg, 73–106. Washington, D.C.: American Enterprise Institute.

Bregger, John E. 1963. "Self-Employment in the United States, 1948–62." *Monthly Labor Review* 86 (January): 37–43.

Brock, William A., David S. Evans, and Bruce D. Phillips. 1986. *The Economics of Small Businesses: Their Role and Regulation in the U.S. Economy.* New York: Holmes and Meier.

Brown, Gary D. 1976. "How Type of Employment Affects Earnings Differences by Sex." *Monthly Labor Review* 99 (July): 25–30.

Bureau of National Affairs. n.d. *Labor Relations Reporter: Wages and Hours Manual.* Washington, D.C.: Bureau of National Affairs.

Burgess, John. 1988. *Self-Employment Growth: An Overview of the Recent Australian Experience.* Department of Economics Occasional Paper no. 149. New South Wales, Aust.: University of Newcastle.

Carroll, Glenn R., and Elaine Mosakowski. 1987. "The Career Dynamics of Self-Employment." *Administrative Science Quarterly* 32 (December): 570–89.

Carson, Carol S. 1984. "The Underground Economy: An Introduction." *Survey of Current Business* 64 (May): 21–37.

Carson, Deane, ed. 1973. *The Vital Majority: Small Business in the American Economy.* Washington, D.C.: Government Printing Office.

Carter, Sara, and Tom Cannon. 1988. *Female Entrepreneurs.* Research Paper no. 65. London: Department of Employment.

Casson, Mark. 1982. *The Entrepreneur and Economic Theory.* Totowa, N.J.: Barnes & Noble.

Chamot, Dennis, and John L. Zalusky. 1985. "Uses and Misuses of Workstations at Home." In National Research Council, Board on Telecommunications and Computer Applications, *Office Workstations in the Home,* 76–84. Washington, D.C.: National Academy Press.

Chase, Anthony G. 1973. "Federal Support of the Vital Majority: The Development of the U.S. Small Business Administration." In *The Vital Majority: Small Business in the American Economy,* ed. Deane Carson, 3–24. Washington, D.C.: Government Printing Office.

Chinoy, Ely. 1955. *Automobile Workers and the American Dream.* New York: Doubleday.

Chiswick, Barry R. 1982. *The Employment of Immigrants in the United States.* Washington, D.C.: American Enterprise Institute.

Clutterbuck, David, ed. 1985. *New Patterns of Work.* New York: St. Martin's Press.

Cole, Richard J., and Philip D. Tegeler. 1980. *Government Requirements of Small Business.* Lexington, Mass.: Lexington Books.

Commerce Clearing House. n.d. *Unemployment Insurance Reporter,* vol. 1B. Chicago: Commerce Clearing House.

Commission of the European Communities. 1987. *Non-Salaried Working Women in Europe.* Luxembourg: Commission of the European Communities.

Covick, Owen. 1983. "Self-Employment Growth in Australia." In *Understanding Labour Markets in Australia,* ed. Richard Blandy and Owen Covick, 84–110. Sydney, Aust.: Allen & Unwin.

Creigh, Stephen, Ceridwen Roberts, Andrea Gorman, and Paul Sawyer. 1986. "Self-Employment in Britain." *Employment Gazette* 94 (June): 183–94.

Cromie, Stanley. 1987. "Motivations of Aspiring Male and Female Entrepreneurs." *Journal of Occupational Behaviour* 8 (July): 251–62.

Cullen, John B. 1978. *The Structure of Professionalism.* New York: Petrocelli.

Cummings, Scott, ed. 1980. *Self-Help in Urban America: Patterns of Minority Business Enterprise.* Port Washington, N.Y.: Kennikat Press.

Daum, Menachem. 1984. "Correlates and Consequences of Salaried and Self-Employment in Mid and Late Life." Brookdale Center on Aging, Hunter College. Typescript.

David, A. M. 1973. *Pensions Insurance of Self-Employed Persons Other than Farmers.* Geneva: International Social Security Association.

Derber, Charles, ed. 1982. *Professionals as Workers: Mental Labor in Advanced Capitalism.* Boston: G. K. Hall.

Doctors, Samuel I., ed. 1974. *Whatever Happened to Minority Economic Development?* Hinsdale, Ill.: Dryden Press.

Doctors, Samuel I., and Vita T. Appel. 1974. "Nixon's Minority Capitalism Program: Full Steam to Where?" In *Whatever Happened to Minority Economic Development?,* ed. Samuel I. Doctors, 109–19. Hinsdale, Ill.: Dryden Press.

Douglas, Paul H. 1957. *The Theory of Wages.* New York: Kelly & Millman.

Eden, Dov. 1975. "Organizational Membership vs. Self-Employment: Another Blow to the American Dream." *Organizational Behavior and Human Performance* 13: 79–94.

Ehrenberg, Ronald G., and Robert S. Smith. 1991. *Modern Labor Economics: Theory and Public Policy,* 4th ed. New York: HarperCollins.

Elfring, Tom. 1988. *Service Sector Employment in Advanced Economies: A Comparative Analysis of Its Implications for Economic Growth.* Hants, Eng.: Avebury (Gower).

Elisburg, Donald. 1985. "Legalities." In National Research Council, Board on Telecommunications and Computer Applications, *Office Workstations in the Home,* 59–65. Washington, D.C.: National Academy Press.

Elliott, Margaret, and Grace E. Manson. 1930. *Earnings of Women in Business and the Professions.* Ann Arbor: Bureau of Business Research, School of Business Administration, University of Michigan.

Employment Gazette. 1989. Historical Suppl. no. 2. Employment Statistics.

Evans, David G., and Linda Leighton. 1987. *Self-Employment Selection and Earnings over the Life Cycle.* Bronx, N.Y.: Department of Economics, Fordham University.

———. 1989. "Some Empirical Aspects of Entrepreneurship." *American Economic Review* 79 (June): 519–35.

Evans, M. D. R. 1989. "Immigrant Entrepreneurship: Effects of Ethnic Market Size and Isolated Labor Pool." *American Sociological Review* 54 (December): 950–62.

Evans, Robert G. 1980. "Professionals and the Production Function: Can Competition Policy Improve Efficiency in the Licensed Professionals?" In *Occupational Licensure and Regulation*, ed. Simon Rottenberg, 229–64. Washington, D.C.: American Enterprise Institute.

Fain, T. Scott. 1980. "Self-Employed Americans: Their Number Has Increased." *Monthly Labor Review* 103 (November): 3–8.

Fanning, Connell M., and Thomas McCarthy. 1986. "A Survey of Economic Hypotheses Concerning the Non-Viability of Labour-Directed Firms in Capitalist Economies." In *Labour-Owned Firms and Workers' Cooperatives*, ed. Sune Jansson and Ann-Britt Hellmark, 7–50. Aldershot, Eng.: Gower.

Feige, Edgar L. 1979. "How Big Is the Irregular Economy?" *Challenge* 22 (November–December): 5–13.

Feinstein, C. H. 1968. "Changes in the Distribution of the National Income in the United Kingdom since 1860." In *The Distribution of National Income*, ed. Jean Marchal and Bernard Ducros, 115–48. London: St. Martin's Press.

Form, William H. 1985. *Divided We Stand: Working-Class Stratification in America*. Urbana: University of Illinois Press.

Fratoe, Frank A. 1986. "A Sociological Analysis of Minority Business." *Review of Black Political Economy* 15 (Fall): 5–30.

Fredland, J. Eric, and Roger D. Little. 1981. "Self-Employed Workers: Returns to Education and Training." *Economics of Education Review* 1 (Summer): 315–37.

————. 1985. "Psychic Income and Self-Employment." *Journal of Private Enterprise* 1 (Fall): 121–26.

Freeman, Richard B. 1980. "The Effect of Occupational Licensure on Black Occupational Attainment." In *Occupational Licensure and Regulation*, ed. Simon Rottenberg, 165–79. Washington, D.C.: American Enterprise Institute.

Freidson, Eliot. 1986. *Professional Powers: A Study of the Institutionalization of Formal Knowledge*. Chicago: University of Chicago Press.

Friedman, Milton, and Simon Kuznets. 1954. *Income from Independent Professional Practice*. New York: National Bureau of Economic Research.

Fuchs, Victor R. 1968. *The Service Economy*. New York: National Bureau of Economic Research.

————. 1971. "Differences in Hourly Earnings between Men and Women." *Monthly Labor Review* 94 (May): 9–15.

————. 1982. "Self-Employment and Labor Force Participation of Older Males." *Journal of Human Resources* 17 (Summer): 339–57.

Gaertner, Wolf, and Alois Wenig, eds. 1985. *The Economics of the Shadow Economy*. Berlin and Heidelberg: Springer-Verlag.

Garvin, Wilfred J. 1973. "Fostering Minority Business Ownership." In *The Vital Majority: Small Business in the American Economy*, ed. Deane Carson, 405–34. Washington, D.C.: Government Printing Office.

Gellhorn, Walter. 1976. "The Abuse of Occupational Licensing." *University of Chicago Law Review* 44 (Fall): 6–27.

Gilb, Corinne L. 1966. *Hidden Hierarchies: The Professions and Government*. New York: Harper & Row.

Gill, Colin. 1985. *Work, Unemployment and the New Technology.* Cambridge, Eng.: Polity Press.

Ginzberg, Eli, Timothy J. Noyelle, and Thomas M. Stanback, Jr. 1986. *Technology and Employment: Concepts and Clarifications.* Boulder, Colo.: Westview Press.

Gordus, Jeanne P., Paul Jarley, and Louis A. Ferman. 1981. *Plant Closings and Economic Dislocation.* Kalamazoo, Mich.: W. E. Upjohn Institute for Employment Research.

Gould, Carole. 1988. "The Embattled Professional Corporation." *New York Times,* October 23.

Grayson, Paul. 1982. "Individual Income Tax Returns: Selected Characteristics from the 1980 Taxpayer Usage Study." *Statistics of Income Bulletin* 1: 13–20.

Gutmann, Peter M. 1979. "Statistical Illusions, Mistaken Policies." *Challenge* 22 (November–December): 14–17.

Haber, Sheldon E., Eugene J. Lamas, and Jules Lichtenstein. 1987. "On Their Own: The Self-Employed and Others in Private Business." *Monthly Labor Review* 110 (May): 17–23.

Haber, William, Louis A. Ferman, and James R. Hudson. 1963. *The Impact of Technological Change.* Kalamazoo, Mich.: W. E. Upjohn Institute of Employment Research.

Hakim, Catherine. 1989. "New Recruits to Self-Employment in the 1980s." *Employment Gazette* 97 (June): 286–97.

Hamermesh, Daniel S. 1990. "Shirking or Productive Schmoozing: Wages and the Allocation of Time at Work." *Industrial and Labor Relations Review* 43 (February): 121S–33S.

Hebert, F. Ted, and Fred W. Becker. 1985. "Preferential Treatment for Small Businesses in Federal Contract Awards." *Policy Studies Journal* 13 (June): 756–65.

Henry, Stuart, ed. 1981. *Can I Have It in Cash?* London: Astragal Books.

Hicks, John R. 1966. *The Theory of Wages.* 2d ed. London: Macmillan.

Highfield, Richard, and Robert Smiley. 1986. "New Business Starts and Economic Activity: An Empirical Investigation." Johnson Graduate School of Management, Cornell University. Typescript.

Hinds, Michael deCourcy. 1990. "Door to a Business of One's Own Can Be Good Exit from Welfare." *New York Times,* June 3.

Holen, Arlene S. 1965. "Effects of Professional Licensing Arrangements on Interstate Labor Mobility and Resource Allocation." *Journal of Political Economy* 73 (October): 492–98.

Horowitz, Ira. 1980. "The Economic Foundation of Self-Regulation in the Professions." In *Regulating the Professions,* ed. Roger D. Blair and Stephen Rubin, 3–28. Lexington, Mass.: Lexington Books.

Horvath, Francis W. 1983. "Job Tenure of Workers in January 1981." In BLS Bulletin no. 2162, *Job Tenure and Occupational Change, 1981,* 1–3. Washington, D.C.: Government Printing Office.

———. 1986. "Work at Home: New Findings from the Current Population Survey." *Monthly Labor Review* 109 (November): 31–35.

Iams, Howard M. 1987. "Jobs of Persons Working after Receiving Retired Worker Benefits." *Social Security Bulletin* 50 (November): 4–19.

International Labour Office. 1990. *The Promotion of Self-Employment.* Geneva: International Labour Office.

International Social Security Association. 1981. "The Social Protection of Self-Employed Workers." Report prepared for the European Regional Meeting on the Social Protection of Self-Employed Non-Agricultural Workers, Paris.

Jansson, Sune, and Ann-Britt Hellmark, eds. 1986. *Labour-Owned Firms and Worker's Cooperatives.* Aldershot, Eng.: Gower.

Johnson, Peter. 1981. "Unemployment and Self-Employment: A Survey." *Industrial Relations Journal* 12 (September–October): 5–15.

Johnson, William R. 1977. "Uncertainty and the Distribution of Earnings." In *The Distribution of Economic Well-Being,* ed. F. Thomas Juster, 375–96. Cambridge, Mass.: Ballinger.

"Judge Backs Rule on Work at Home." 1989. *New York Times,* December 8.

Kehrer, Barbara. 1976. "Factors Affecting the Incomes of Men and Women Physicians: An Exploratory Analysis." *Journal of Human Resources* 11 (Fall): 526–45.

Kennedy, Liam, ed. 1983. *Economic Theory of Cooperative Enterprises: Selected Readings.* Oxford, Eng.: Plunkett Foundation for Cooperative Studies.

Kilborn, Peter T. 1990. "Novel Program for the Jobless Aims to Create Entrepreneurs." *New York Times,* May 16.

Knight, Frank H. 1933. *Risk, Uncertainty and Profit.* London: London School of Economics and Political Science.

Kotkin, Joel. 1986. "The Reluctant Entrepreneurs." *Inc.* 8 (September): 81–89.

Lawson, Carol. 1985. "Aid for Women Starting Businesses." *New York Times,* August 1.

Lebergott, Stanley. 1964. *Manpower in Economic Growth: The United States Record since 1800.* New York: Macmillan.

Lee, Raymond. 1985. "The Entry to Self-Employment of Redundant Steelworkers." *Industrial Relations Journal* 16 (Summer): 42–49.

Leveson, Irving F. 1968. "Nonfarm Self-Employment in the United States." Ph.D. dissertation, Columbia University.

Levy, Marcia. 1975. *Self-Employment in the Covered Workforce.* Staff Paper no. 19. Washington, D.C.: Department of Health, Education, and Welfare.

Lichtenstein, Jules H. 1989. "Measuring Self-Employment as a Micro-Business Phenomenon." Paper presented at international conference, "The Self-Employment Strategy: Building the New Economy," Toronto, October 18–20.

Lichtenstein, Peter M. 1986. "The Concept of the Firm in the Economic Theory of 'Alternative Organizations': Appraisal and Reformulation." In *Labour-Owned Firms and Workers' Cooperatives,* ed. Sune Jansson and Ann-Britt Hellmark, 51–72. Aldershot, Eng.: Gower.

Light, Ivan. 1980. "Asian Enterprise in America." In *Self-Help in Urban America: Patterns of Minority Business Enterprise,* ed. Scott Cummings, 33–57. Port Washington, N.Y.: Kennikat Press.

Light, Ivan, and Edna Bonacich. 1988. *Immigrant Entrepreneurs: Koreans in Los Angeles, 1965–1982.* Berkeley: University of California Press.

Linder, Marc. 1983. "Self-Employment as a Cyclical Escape from Unemployment: A Case Study of the Construction Industry in the United States during the Postwar Period." In *Research in the Sociology of Work: Peripheral Workers,* vol. 2, ed. Ida Harper Simpson and Richard L. Simpson, 261–74. Greenwich, Conn.: JAI Press.

Little Roger D., 1990. "Gender Differences in Human Capital Returns to Self-Employment." Paper presented at meetings of the Eastern Economics Association, Cincinnati, March 31.

Long, James E. 1982. "The Income Tax and Self-Employment." *National Tax Journal* 35 (March): 31–42.

Lovell-Troy, Lawrence A. 1980. "Clan Structure and Economic Activity: The Case of Greeks in Small Business Enterprise." In *Self-Help in Urban America: Patterns of Minority Business Enterprise,* ed. Scott Cummings, 58–88. Port Washington, N.Y.: Kennikat Press.

Lozano, Beverly. 1989. *The Invisible Work Force.* New York: Free Press.

McCrohan, Kevin F., and James D. Smith. 1983. "Informal Suppliers in the Underground Economy." *Statistics of Income Bulletin* 3 (Summer): 27–33.

McDonald, Richard J. 1984. "The 'Underground Economy' and BLS Statistical Data." *Monthly Labor Review* 107 (January): 4–18.

McKay, Steven F. 1989. *Short-Range Actuarial Projections of the Old-Age Survivors and Disability Insurance Program, 1988.* Washington, D.C.: U.S. Social Security Administration, Office of the Actuary.

Mangum, Stephen L., and Judy Tansky. 1988. "Self-Employment Training as an Intervention Strategy for Displaced or Disadvantaged Workers." In *Proceedings of the Fortieth Annual Meeting of the Industrial Relations Research Association,* 346–55. Madison, Wisc.: Industrial Relations Research Association.

Marchal, Jean, and Bernard Ducros, eds. 1968. *The Distribution of National Income.* London: St. Martin's Press.

Marshall, Alfred. 1898. *Principles of Economics,* vol. 1. 4th ed. London: Macmillan.

Mattera, Philip. 1985. *Off the Books: The Rise of the Underground Economy.* New York: St. Martin's Press.

Mayer, Kurt B., and Sidney Goldstein. 1964. "Manual Workers as Small Businessmen." In *Blue-Collar World,* ed. Arthur B. Shostak and William Gomberg, 537–49. New York: Prentice-Hall.

Mayers, Kenneth E. 1978. "In the Red in Black and White: A Policy Analysis of Black Capitalism in the Light of White Small Business." Ph.D. dissertation, University of California, Berkeley.

Meade, James E. 1975. "The Theory of Labour-Managed Firms and of Profit-Sharing." In *Self-Management: Economic Liberation of Man,* ed. Jaroslav Vanek, 394–422. Baltimore: Penguin.

Moore, Robert L. 1983. "Employer Discrimination: Evidence from Self-Employed Workers." *Review of Economics and Statistics* 65 (August): 496–501.

Myrdal, Gunnar. 1944. *An American Dilemma: The Negro Problem and Modern Democracy.* New York: Harper.

National Research Council. Board on Telecommunications and Computer Applications. Commission on Engineering and Technical Systems. 1985. *Office Workstations in the Home.* Washington, D.C.: National Academy Press.

New York State Department of Commerce. Division for Small Business. n.d. *Your Business: A Management Guide for Small, Minority and Women-Owned Businesses.* Albany.

New York State Office of Business Permits. 1987. *1986 Annual Report.* Albany.

Nieuwenhuysen, John, and Marina Williams-Wynn. 1982. *Professions in the Marketplace.* Melbourne: Melbourne University Press.

Oaxaca, Ronald L. 1973. "Male-Female Wage Differentials in Urban Labor Markets." *International Economic Review* 14: 693–709.

O'Higgins, Michael. 1980. "Measuring Tax Evasion: A Review of Evidence and Methodologies." Centre for Fiscal Studies, University of Bath. Typescript.

———. 1985. "The Relationship between the Formal and Hidden Economies: An Exploratory Analysis for Four Countries." In *The Economics of the Shadow Economy,* ed. Wolf Gaertner and Alois Wenig, Berlin and Heidelberg: Springer-Verlag.

Organization for Economic Cooperation and Development. 1985. *Labour Force Statistics: 1963–1983.* Paris.

———. 1986. *Employment Outlook.* Paris.

Ostry, Sylvia. 1978. "Competition Policy and the Self-Regulating Profession." In *The Professions and Public Policy,* ed. Philip Slayton and Michael J. Trebilcock, 17–29. Toronto: University of Toronto Press.

Oxenfeldt, Alfred R. 1943. *New Firms and Free Enterprise.* Washington, D.C.: American Council on Public Affairs.

Palen, J. John, and Frank J. Fahey. 1968. "Unemployment and Reemployment Success: An Analysis of the Studebaker Shutdown." *Industrial and Labor Relations Review* 21 (January): 234–50.

Parnes, Herbert S., and Lawrence J. Less. 1985. "Economic Well-Being in Retirement." In *Retirement among American Men,* ed. Herbert S. Parnes, 91–118. Lexington, Mass.: Lexington Books.

Pashigian, B. Peter. 1979. "Occupational Licensing and the Interstate Mobility of Professionals." *Journal of Law and Economics* 22 (April): 1–25.

———. 1980. "Has Occupational Licensing Reduced Geographical Mobility and Raised Earnings?" In *Occupational Licensure and Regulation,* ed. Simon Rottenberg, 299–333. Washington, D.C.: American Enterprise Institute.

Passel, Peter. 1990. "Small Business, Large Mirage." *New York Times,* May 9.

Phillips, Joseph D. 1958. *Little Business in the American Economy.* Urbana: University of Illinois Press.

———. 1962. *The Self-Employed in the United States.* Urbana: University of Illinois.

Portes, Alejandro, and Leif Jensen. 1987. "Comment." *American Sociological Review* 52 (December): 768–71.

———. 1989. "The Enclave and the Entrants: Patterns of Ethnic Enterprise in Miami before and after Mariel." *American Sociological Review* 54 (December): 929–49.

Quinn, Joseph F. 1980. "Labor Force Participation Patterns of Older Self-Employed Workers." *Social Security Bulletin* 43 (April): 17–28.

Rasmussen, P. Norregard. 1968. "On the Interrelationship between Growth and the Distribution of Income." In *The Distribution of National Income,* ed. Jean Marchal and Bernard Ducros, 511–38. London: St. Martin's Press.

Ray, Robert N. 1975. "Self-Employed Americans in 1973." *Monthly Labor Review* 98 (January): 49–54.

Rayack, Elton. 1975. *An Economic Analysis of Occupational Licensure.* Washington, D.C.: U.S. Department of Labor, Office of Research and Development.

Roberts, Sam. 1990. "Turning Boycott of Greengrocer into Green Power." *New York Times,* June 7.

Rottenberg, Simon, ed. 1980. *Occupational Licensure and Regulation.* Washington, D.C.: American Enterprise Institute.

Russell, Raymond. 1985. *Sharing Ownership in the Workplace.* Albany: SUNY Press.

Sanborn, Henry. 1964. "Pay Differences between Men and Women." *Industrial and Labor Relations Review* 17: 534–50.

Sanders, Jimy M., and Victor Nee. 1987. "Limits of Ethnic Solidarity in the Enclave Economy." *American Sociological Review* 52 (December): 745–67.

Scase, Richard, and Robert Goffee. 1982. *The Entrepreneurial Middle Class.* London: Croom Helm.

Schumpeter, Joseph A. 1934. *The Theory of Economic Development: An Inquiry into Profits, Capital, and Credit.* Cambridge: Harvard University Press.

"Self-Employment: A Way to Ease the Jobs Crisis?" 1990. *ILO Information* 18 (May): 1, 6.

Shimberg, Benjamin. 1985. "Overview of Professional and Occupational Licensing." In *Understanding Testing in Occupational Licensing,* ed. Jim C. Fortune, 1–14. San Francisco: Jossey-Bass.

Shimberg, Benjamin, Barbara F. Esser, and Daniel H. Kruger. 1972. *Occupational Licensing: Practices and Policies.* Washington, D.C.: Public Affairs Press.

Silvestri, George, and John Lukesiewicz. 1989. "Projections of Occupational Employment, 1988–2000." *Monthly Labor Review* 112 (November): 42–65.

Simon, Carl P., and Ann D. Witte. 1982. *Beating the System: The Underground Economy.* Boston: Auburn House.

Slayton, Philip, and Michael J. Trebilcock, eds. 1978. *The Professions and Public Policy.* Toronto: University of Toronto Press.

Smith, Stephen. 1986. *Britain's Shadow Economy.* Oxford: Clarendon Press.

Solomon, Steven. 1986. *Small Business U.S.A.* New York: Crown.

Sonfield, Matthew C. 1976. "Entrepreneurship in Black and White: An Attitudinal Comparison of Black and White Small Businessmen." Ph.D. dissertation, New York University Graduate School of Business Administration.

Sowell, Thomas. 1981. *Markets and Minorities.* New York: Basic Books.

Stanback, Thomas M., Jr. 1979. *Understanding the Service Economy.* Baltimore: Johns Hopkins University Press.

Statistical Office of the European Communities. 1986. *Labour Force Survey Results, 1984.* Luxembourg.

Statistisches Bundesamt. 1982. *Stand und Entwicklung der Erwerbstätigkeit.* Wiesbaden: Fachseriel.

Steinmetz, George, and Erik Olin Wright. 1989. "The Fall and Rise of the Petty Bourgeoisie: Changing Patterns of Self-Employment in the Postwar United States." *American Journal of Sociology* 94 (March): 973–1018.

Taubman, Paul. 1975. *Sources of Inequality in Earnings: Personal Skills, Random Events, Preferences toward Risks, and Other Occupational Characteristics.* New York: American Elsevier Press.

Thompson, Daniel C. 1986. *A Black Elite: A Profile of Graduates of United Negro College Fund Colleges.* Westport, Conn.: Greenwood Press.

Tschetter, John. 1987. "Producer Services: Why Are They Growing So Rapidly?" *Monthly Labor Review* 110 (December): 31–40.

"Two Years after the Enterprise Allowance Scheme." 1986. *Employment Gazette* 94 (October): 405–8.

U.S. Bureau of the Census. 1953. *U.S. Census of Population, 1950. Detailed Characteristics. U.S. Summary.* Washington, D.C.: Government Printing Office.

———. 1973. Occupational Characteristics. *U.S. Census of Population, 1970, Subject Reports,* vol. 2. Washington, D.C.: Government Printing Office.

———. 1974. Consumer Income. *Current Population Reports,* ser. P-60, no. 95. Washington, D.C.: Government Printing Office.

———. 1981. Consumer Income. *Current Population Reports,* ser. P-60, no. 130. Washington, D.C.: Government Printing Office.

———. 1984a. *U.S. Census of Population, 1980. Detailed Characteristics. U.S. Summary.* Washington, D.C.: Government Printing Office.

———. 1984b. Consumer Income. *Current Population Reports,* ser. P-60, no. 142. Washington, D.C.: Government Printing Office.

———. 1984c. Occupation by Industry. *U.S. Census of Population, 1980, Subject Reports.* Washington, D.C.: Government Printing Office.

———. 1984–85. *1982 Survey of Minority-Owned Business Enterprises.* Washington, D.C.: Government Printing Office.

———. 1985. Money Income of Households, Families, and Persons in the United States, 1983. *Current Population Reports,* ser. P-60, no. 146. Washington, D.C.: Government Printing Office.

———. 1987. *1982 Characteristics of Business Owners.* Washington, D.C.: Government Printing Office.

U.S. Congress. Select Commission on Immigration and Refugee Policy. 1980. *Semiannual Report.* Washington, D.C.: Government Printing Office.

U.S. Department of Commerce. Bureau of Industrial Economics. 1987. *Franchising in the Economy, 1983–85.* Washington, D.C.: Government Printing Office.

U.S. Department of Health and Human Services. Social Security Administration. Various years. *Social Security Bulletin, Annual Statistical Supplements.* Washington, D.C.: Government Printing Office.

U.S. Department of Labor. Bureau of Labor Statistics. Various years. *Employment and Earnings.* Washington, D.C.: Government Printing Office.

———. 1982. *Labor Force Statistics Derived from the Current Population Survey.* Bulletin 2096. Washington, D.C.: Government Printing Office.

———. 1985. *Handbook of Labor Statistics.* Bulletin 2217. Washington, D.C.: Government Printing Office.

————. 1988. *Labor Force Statistics Derived from the Current Population Survey, 1948–87.* Bulletin 2307. Washington, D.C.: Government Printing Office.

U.S. General Accounting Office. 1981. *Using the Exact Match File for Estimates and Characteristics of Persons Reporting and Not Reporting Social Security Self-Employment Earnings.* Report of the Chairman, Subcommittee on Oversight, House Committee on Ways and Means. Washington, D.C.: Government Printing Office.

U.S. President. 1988. *Economic Report of the President: February 1988.* Washington, D.C.: Government Printing Office.

U.S. Small Business Administration. Office of Advocacy. 1984–89. *The State of Small Business: A Report of the President.* Annual Report. Washington, D.C.: Government Printing Office.

————. 1988. *Small Business in the American Economy.* Washington, D.C.: Government Printing Office.

U.S. Treasury Department. 1978. *Credit and Capital Formation: A Report to the President's Interagency Task Force on Women Business Owners.* Washington, D.C.: Government Printing Office.

————. 1977, 1980, 1982, 1983, 1984. Sole Proprietors. *Statistics of Income Bulletin.* Washington, D.C.: Government Printing Office.

Vanek, Jaroslav, ed. 1975. *Self-Management: Economic Liberation of Man.* Baltimore: Penguin.

Weingast, Barry. 1980. "Physicians, DNA Research Scientists, and the Market for Lemons." In *Regulating the Professions,* ed. Roger D. Blair and Stephen Rubin, 81–96. Lexington, Mass.: Lexington Books.

Wolfson, Alan D., Michael J. Trebilcock, and Carolyn J. Tuohy. 1980. "Regulating the Professions: A Theoretical Framework." In *Occupational Licensure and Regulation,* ed. Simon Rottenberg, 180–204. Washington, D.C.: American Enterprise Institute.

Wolpin, Kenneth I. 1977. "Education and Screening." *American Economic Review* 67 (December): 949–58.

Wright, Erik Olin. 1979. *Class Structure and Income Determination.* New York: Academic Press.

Young, S. David. 1985. *The Rule of Experts: Occupational Licensing in America.* Washington, D.C.: Cato Institute.

Yuengert, Andrew M. 1989. *Self-Employment and the Earnings of Male Immigrants in the U.S.* Economic Growth Center Discussion Paper no. 581, Yale University.

Zhou, Min, and John R. Logan. 1989. "Returns on Human Capital in Ethnic Enclaves: New York City's Chinatown." *American Sociological Review* 54 (October): 809–20.

Index

ABOUT THE AUTHOR

Robert L. Aronson holds bachelor's and master's degrees from Ohio State University and a Ph.D. from Princeton University. He joined the faculty of the School of Industrial and Labor Relations at Cornell University in 1950 and was made an emeritus professor in 1983. His principal research interests are the impact of industrial and technological change on labor markets, the employment effects of plant shutdowns, occupational mobility, and the unionization of professional workers.